Jesus:
INSPIRING AND DISTURBING PRESENCE

Y0-BDM-967

Jesus:
INSPIRING AND DISTURBING PRESENCE

M. de Jonge

Translated by John E. Steely

ABINGDON PRESS
Nashville —— New York

BRESCIA COLLEGE
LIBRARY
38045

JEZUS: INSPIRATOR EN SPELBREKER
copyright © 1971 Uitgeverij G. F. Callenbach N. V.

JESUS: INSPIRING AND DISTURBING PRESENCE
translation © 1974 by Abingdon Press

All rights reserved.

Library of Congress Cataloging in Publication Data
JONGE, MARINUS de, 1925-
  Jesus: Inspiring and Disturbing Presence
  Translation of Jezus, inspirator en spelbreker
  Includes bibliographical references
  1. Jesus Christ—Person and offices—Addresses,
    essays, lectures. I. Title.
  BT202.J6513   232   74-10915

ISBN 0-687-19919-0
ISBN 0-687-19920-4 paper

Quotation on p. 72 is from Albert Camus, *The Fall,* trans. by Justin O'Brien (New York: Alfred A. Knopf, 1957).

Quotations on pp. 96, 169 are from Paul van Buren, *The Secular Meaning of the Gospel,* © 1963 by Macmillan Publishing Company.

Quotations on pp. 39-40 are from Albert Schweitzer, *The Quest of the Historical Jesus* © 1906 by Macmillan Publishing Company.

Quotations on pp. 102, 108, 109 are from "Murke's Collected Silences" by Heinrich Boll. Copyright 1971 by McGraw-Hill Book Company. Used with permission of McGraw-Hill Book Company.

Quotation on p. 58 is from *Honest to God,* by John A. T. Robinson. Published in the U.S.A. by The Westminster Press, 1963. © SCM Press, Ltd., 1963. Used by Permission.

Quotations on p. 111 are from *Situation Ethics,* by Joseph Fletcher. Copyright © MCMLXVI, W. L. Jenkins. Used by permission of The Westminster Press.

Quotations from A. M. Wilder, *The Language of the Gospel: Early Christian Rhetoric,* are used by permission of Harper & Row Publishers, Inc.

Quotations on pp. 11-12, 13 are from Gerrit Achterberg, "Deisme," and are used by permission of Mevr. J. C. Achterberg-van Baak.

Quotations on p. 31 are from *Images of the Church in the New Testament,* by Paul S. Minear. Copyright © MCMLX, W. L. Jenkins. Used by permission of The Westminster Press.

Scripture quotations noted RSV are from the Revised Standard Version of the Bible, copyrighted 1946, 1952, and 1971, by the Division of Christian Education, National Council of Churches, and are used by permission.

Scripture quotations noted NEB are from The New English Bible, © the Delegates of the Oxford University Press and the Syndics of the Cambridge University Press 1961, 1970. Reprinted by permission.

MANUFACTURED BY THE PARTHENON PRESS AT
NASHVILLE, TENNESSEE, UNITED STATES OF AMERICA

Contents

Translator's Preface

It is a pleasure to have a share in bringing to a wider reading public the work of Dr. M. de Jonge, who is professor of New Testament at the University of Leiden, the Netherlands. Readers will be prompted by his thought to reflect in a new way upon old issues and to consider questions which had never occurred to them. What he has to offer for both the intellectual and the devotional life of our time will, I believe, be evident in the following pages.

To Professor de Jonge I should like to express thanks for his kind encouragement to me in this undertaking and for the prompt and helpful response to my questions. While he has seen the translation, the responsibility for any failure to set forth his meaning is mine.

This preface affords an opportunity also to express gratitude for the friendship and support, in unnamed and unnumbered ways, of Dr. William T. Flynt over a span of many years. He, too, as a disciple of this Jesus who is the center of this book, has been for many both *inspirator* and *spelbreker* (to use the words of the book's title in Dutch). Finally, for my family's help and encouragement, my warmest and most constant gratitude must be expressed—an obligation that is also privilege.

JOHN E. STEELY
Wake Forest, N.C.
January, 1974

I
On Weighing Our Words

Introduction

This book is a collection of a number of articles which have appeared in past years in various journals, supplemented by some essays that have not been published heretofore. All the chapters are concerned, from varying perspectives, with the question of the right translation of the message of Jesus, and with the proclamation concerning him, into the words and deeds of the present time.

Some parts were written when it was necessary to warn against a too massive word-theology and a glorification of certain biblical or Reformation terms and concepts. Other expositions are aimed directly against a too glib and too uncritical use of modern terminology. Current images and concepts—whether they are traditional or modern—are not at once usable for handing on what is unique in the message of God in Jesus of Nazareth. They must be taken in their limitations and at the same time must be shattered. Proclamation needs to use the ordinary language of ordinary people because otherwise there is no genuine communication. At the same time it must be evident that the ordinary terms must be recoined, so that what is distinctive and unique about this message can be handed on.

What is true of our words applies likewise to our deeds. The imitation of Jesus does not consist in repetition and mimicry, but in obedient and creative seeking for the way which must be taken now. This never coincides with the accepted Christian morality; just as little does it coincide with the latest ethical or political "ism" of the day. In Jesus' summons to love, every commandment is radicalized and at the same time relativized. Jesus himself took the ultimate step in his love, out of a divine compulsion, and he draws others with him in the process of renewal that he has set in motion in this world. Therefore following after Jesus is characterized by being radical without being convulsive.

In the present volume no closed system of thought or action is offered. It gives a limited number of variations on one central theme. The title expresses the fact that orientation to Jesus of Nazareth is indispensable for every Christian and for every form of common Christian life and thought. At the same time, it means to say that it is a marvel that after nineteen hundred years this man among men still constantly inspires people to search for new words and new deeds. But along with his being an inspiring presence, Jesus is also a disturbing presence; just when a man thinks he knows it all, builds his doctrinal system, or establishes himself on an ethical code, then what he has is taken from him, then he is sent out to search for new words and to experiment with new norms.

In these days there is much that is being demolished and is disappearing; at the same time there is a great deal of experimentation. We are not very happy with what is ancient, and we are unsure of what is new; renewal quickly degenerates into a radical overthrowing of the old, and maintenance of tradition becomes a convulsive rejection of all that is new. Yet it must be possible to go forward in the line of history, honest with God, honest with our fellowmen, honest with ourselves, and avoiding the extremes of reaction and revolution. Orientation to Jesus, inspirer and

10

troubler, is necessary for everyone, regardless of where he is and what his ties are.

These studies are written by an exegete who is interested in dogmatic and ethical questions, one who is occupied in scholarly work on the Bible, especially the New Testament, and who constantly tries to ask how he now must put into words and can translate into deeds what is found in the Bible.

Therewith the limitations of what is offered here are clearly indicated. The emphasis lies upon what is given in the New Testament. Again and again the effort is made to emphasize that there are many more starting points to be found for a modern theology and a modern ethic than people usually think. The lines which are drawn to the present day are nothing more than dotted lines; the author hopes that they will yet be so clearly marked that others will draw them in completely. Theology can sensibly be pursued only as teamwork. Seeking for new words and for responsible action is, moreover, not a task for theologians alone, but a mandate for all Christians.

An example: Jesus as Shepherd and as Junkman

The following poem was published by the poet Gerrit Achterberg under the title "Deism" in *Maatstaf:*[1]

> For a while man is a place for God.
> If you take this away from anyone,
> All that is left is a cemetery with a headstone
> Under which lies one who had come to
> This conclusion, this abrupt end.
> But God goes on, sweeps beyond him
> With his millions. God is never alone,
> For he consists of a surplus of life.
>
> For him we are full fuel cans.
> When we are empty he leaves us behind, without regret.

11

Since he moves onward and outward
We die, and lie along the road.

If it were not for the shepherd Jesus Christ,
Who came to find us as lost lambs.

Here is an impressive expression of how great God is and how small is man. Only for a short time man may have a share in the overflowing life of a God who goes on and leaves the man behind like a gravestone in a cemetery or—to change the figure—like an empty fuel can left behind by advancing soldiers on the battlefield.

Dead, man is useless, and God seems no longer to be interested in him. But strangely enough, Jesus Christ comes, and he will find us—the figure changes once again—as a shepherd finds a lost lamb.

In order to express the coming, seeking, and finding by Jesus Christ, whose relationship to God is not precisely defined, Achterberg reaches for the biblical figure of the lost sheep and with it, at the same time, that of the good shepherd. One thinks at once of the parable of the lost sheep in Luke 15:3-7, which places the emphasis on God's joy over the one sinner who repents, and the shepherd's concern for the sheep that has gone astray. Or one thinks of the parallel parable in Matthew 18:12-14, where, as it appears from the concluding sentence and from the context, the shepherd's searching is put forth as an example for Jesus' disciples: God does not will that any one of these "little ones" should be lost. We can also point to John 10:1-21, where the figure of the good shepherd and his flock is worked out most specifically and in the greatest detail. There Jesus very clearly is the unique good shepherd; he has a special relationship of trust to his sheep, because he stands in a special relationship to the Father. He offers his life for his sheep, and therein the Father's love for the people entrusted to Jesus' care comes to expression.

12

Achterberg returned to these New Testament variations on the good shepherd theme when he wanted to indicate how the lost man is sought and found. Yet the transition from the abandoned empty fuel can to the good shepherd and the lost lamb is abrupt. The poet also obviously was not satisfied with it and, as he did so often,[2] he revised this poem. In the volume entitled *Vergeetboek* it reads as follows:[3]

> For a while man is a place for God.
> When an equals-sign no longer keeps things together,
> Then he is written off on a tombstone.
> The agreement seems to move to
> This conclusion, this abrupt end.
>
> For God goes on, swerving away from him
> With his millions. God is never alone.
> There are others bidding for his attention.
>
> For him we are full fuel cans.
> When we are empty, he leaves us behind! He must get rid
>   of it.
> All the refuse that is not in agreement with his true being.
>
> Since he distinguishes himself from the creation,
> We die and lie scattered along the road,
>
> If it were not for Christ, dealer in old junk,
> Who had to find us in just such condition;
> As though he had whispered with the Father.

Several major and minor changes have been introduced. In the context of my presentation, I wish only to point to the alterations in the last three lines. The good shepherd has become a dealer in old junk, and the object of his concern has remained an empty gasoline can. A change in figure is avoided, and yet the same thing is said as in the first version of the poem. I refer to the "had to find," which plainly is connected with Christ's whispered

13

conference with the Father, even though Achterberg puts "as though" before his last clause. This stresses more clearly than in the first version that there is a connection between Jesus Christ at the end and God in the beginning of the poem. Achterberg avoids the figure of the shepherd for Jesus, but now he introduces the figure of the Father (capitalized) for God.

I do not wish to go into possible changes in Achterberg's belief in God between the first and second versions of the poem. It is evident that in a poem that is entitled "Deism," the struggle for a clearer, more transparent use of imagery presupposes a concern with the central religious questions; the former affects the latter, and the latter affects the former. Herein the reader remains, in the last analysis, an outsider; he may, however, note with pleasure that in the struggling for new words a new figure is born, one that opens up some new perspectives for him.

"Christ, dealer in old junk." Is this a figure that will work? Yes, of course, because here it is not a matter of just any junk dealer, but a very special one: one who must find, who is looking just for gasoline cans "in just such condition," one who appears "as though he had made a deal with the Father." Achterberg is concerned with Christ, dealer in old junk, just as the author of John 10 was concerned with Christ, the good shepherd. Out of the motifs which the tradition afforded that author in the figure of the shepherd, he brought forward all sorts of things which now applied particularly to Jesus, and in addition he completed his figure with a number of features which so especially belong to Jesus that it becomes evident that only *one* person has the right to call himself the good shepherd. Jesus places the figure of the shepherd in tension—what is involved is *Christ,* the good shepherd. So also with Achterberg the subject is Christ, the dealer in old junk. The theme is a unique shepherd and a unique junk-man, and the figures are so handled that precisely this "unique" quality can be expressed. The discovery of new figures, the

14

placing under tension of words, is the gift of the poet and likewise the task of the preacher, even when the latter is not a poet. If this is done responsibly—that is, in such a way that the message entrusted to us comes across—then we shall be in a position so to hear the old words and figures that what speaks of God sounds through them. And at the same time we shall have to listen to the language which we share with the people around us so that certain words in this language can be placed in the service of God's message. If that succeeds, if the spark jumps (and this is possible at any moment, with any word, even the most ordinary one), then one may accept this with joy as a gift—of the Holy Spirit, the Bible says.

In this searching for new words we are by no means obliged to think specifically of distinctive, lofty things. In *Licht: Het Evangelie van Johannes* ("Light: The Gospel of John"), an experiment in translation into contemporary Dutch,[4] there stands beside the story of the good shepherd a photograph of a lighthouse which sends its shafts of light through the night. The caption reads, "They enter in through me, and then they are safe," a saying from John 10:9 that follows Jesus' utterance, "I am the door of the sheep." In John 10 the figure of the door stands alongside that of the shepherd and supplements it. In the illustration of this gospel in modern translation, the figure of the door, like that of the good shepherd, is avoided and is replaced by a contemporary figure which speaks a clear message in the Netherlands. And that figure itself in turn evokes new images, like that of the keeper of the lighthouse, of the pilot who, if necessary, risks his life, and of the crew of the lifesaving boat: a well-organized, modern apparatus that is entirely oriented to preserving and saving human life.[5] Why should we not also be able to borrow figures from this in order to put into words what is expressed in John 10 with the figures of the shepherd and the door? In the same way, the Parisian teacher who has her kindergarten class cross a busy street by taking the hand of the first child and having the other children hold fast to each other can be used as a modern illustration of what is said in John 17 by Jesus about the unity of the church.[6] But the point is whether we have eyes to see and ears to hear what then took place in and through and around Jesus of Nazareth and what is happening now.

The Plan of this book

In the second chapter the theme that has been suggested is further worked out. Starting out from remarks by H. Kraemer, J. de Graaf, and E. A. Nida, an attempt is made to indicate how closely woven together the orientation to Jesus of Nazareth and the orientation to the modern world need to be if there is to be any talk of an actual communication between church and world and of a responsible contemporary faith on the part of Christians.

In the third chapter the question is posed as to whether orientation to Jesus of Nazareth is possible. When we read the New Testament, are we truly confronted by him, or do we go no further back than the first century Christians' faith in him and their testimony about him? An explanation is given of how responsible historical investigation proceeds with the available sources, and it is also shown how an analysis of the way Jesus is spoken of in the New Testament can help us in our own speaking of him.

This last point is worked out in the next three chapters. Chapter 4 is concerned with the fourth chapter of J. A. T. Robinson's sensational book entitled *Honest to God,*[7] which is devoted to the person and work of Jesus of Nazareth. The emphasis lies on the point that one cannot avoid speaking figuratively about God and Jesus. This theme recurs in chapter 5 where in relation to A. N. Wilder's *Early Christian Rhetoric,*[8] it is shown how the encounter with Jesus led to a life rooted in faith and how this faith forged its own language, created new figures, and placed old ones under

16

tension in a new way. Poets and prophets—see, for example, Achterberg—can say more with words than philosophers and theologians can find in them by means of cool analysis. A. N. Wilder's theories also stand behind the sixth chapter, which concludes with a plea for theology as narrative.

Thus far the subject is primarily the *wording* of what is experienced in the encounter with Jesus of Nazareth. By way of supplement the seventh chapter speaks of communication in words and in silence. This essay (originally written in English for a Quaker journal) places the emphasis upon the connection between speaking and being silent, both of them indispensable in intercourse among people and between man and God. This chapter not only provides a corrective to the preceding one; it also forms the transition to the two following chapters, both of which have reference to behavior that is inspired by Jesus.

Chapter 8 poses the question whether it is true that love ought to be the only guideline for Christian behavior. On the basis of what is said about love in the First Epistle of John, it can be made perfectly clear that what is involved is nothing less than a love that takes its example from God and is inspired and awakened by him. Moreover, one may not merely play love and commandments or love and morality against one another; in the situation of I John it was necessary to say that love is the fulfilling of the commandment. Strange as it may seem, we *must* love.

Chapter 9 is concerned with the question whether Jesus may be called a revolutionary and whether one may draw on the guidelines of the gospel for revolutionary action by Christians. Here again Jesus appears in a peculiar way to be an inspiring and disturbing presence.

Finally, the book concludes in Chapter 10 with the question of who are "we". The "we" who address us in the Bible and tell what has conquered them call on us not to continue as those addressed outside, but to join them in doing, in living, and in bearing witness. The question is whether we are willing instead of being "you" to become "we," willing to cooperate in the work of handing on the gospel, led by the Holy Spirit, to everyone who will receive it. For everyone, theologian or nontheologian, this means both disengagement and engagement and in every case, orientation to Jesus of Nazareth, inspiring and troubling presence.

The author has done his best to write as simply as possible. Difficult terms are avoided insofar as possible, and quotations from foreign languages are translated in every case. The explanatory footnotes at the end can give further help to those who are interested in the original text of the quotations and in references to the literature, but even the notes have been kept to a minimum. Naturally the articles which were already published earlier were also revised so that unnecessary repetition has been avoided. It is understandable that certain points nevertheless recur again and again; it is a matter of variations on a common theme.

18

II

Honest with God and in Touch with the World

Introduction

A number of years ago, in 1959, former members of the Dutch Reformed seminary engaged, in their work conference at Driebergen, in reflecting on the discussion then going on in the church.[1] They found that renewed theological reflection was urgently needed in order to bring this discussion out of the impasse in which it found itself. After having indicated several points to which the reflection needed to be addressed above all, they remarked: "Advances along this line may be expected only if (a) the study is guided by a concentration on the person and work of Christ and we expect from Christ the salvation that God gives, and if (b) there is self-evidently a maximal openness to the questions of a scientific, social, and human sort, with which we shall be confronted in increasing measure by the 'atomic age' that has dawned."[2]

It appears to me that these points are still of current significance. However, at this moment we shall have to lay the emphasis above all on the point that the things said above are indissolubly joined together. The conversation within the churches and between the churches about the central points of the faith and the conversation between church and world ought reciprocally to affect each other. And this not only in practice, (one is simply beating the air if one does not keep the world in view, and it is precisely the witnessing in the world that causes the division of the church to be felt keenly), but also and above all in principle. This can be made clear in a closer analysis of the concept ''communication.''

Communication

Since Kraemer's little book, *Communicatie, een Tijdvraag,*[3] the word communication has become a popular one in the language of the church in the Netherlands. Kraemer makes a distinction between ''communication of,'' the imparting of a particular message, and ''communication between,'' that is, the connection between persons which is the precondition for an authentic mutual understanding and a genuine transmission of ideas and concepts. He then points out that God, who in the Bible seeks communication with men, does not only give or convey through others items of information about himself, but imparts himself, by his will to be ''God-with us,'' Immanuel. Only on the basis of God's seeking fellowship with us do the communications become intelligible, and in fact there is no other content of the message than just this Immanuel. In the communication between God and man the communication between men is likewise renewed; in the fellowship with God in Christ, interpersonal relationships develop into a genuine, deep fellowship. The community of Christ needs to set an example before the world in this respect. Here too it holds true that the God-with-us leads to the we-with-each-other, and conversely; only if the we-with-each-other is a reality can the message of God-with-us really be given through us. Kraemer calls I John 1:1-4 the Magna Charta of communication in the biblical sense and rightly so. ''What we have seen and heard, that we also announce to you, so that you may have fellowship with us. And *our* fellowship is with the Father and with his Son Jesus Christ'' (vss. 3-4).

In an article entitled ''Kerygma en communicatie'' (''Kerygma and Communication''),[4] J. de Graaf has gone further on the way indicated by Kraemer. Communication *of* and communication *between* are to be distinguished only phenomenologically, he says; ''the introduction of the idea of communication signifies a change *in the entire field of theology and in every aspect of the church's being the church*'' (p. 208). Kerygma, proclamation, occurs only in communication, and this implies that in conversation with the world we not only must change the form of the message, need to modernize our language, need to adjust our vocabulary, and must change the setting (not preaching halls, but, for example, conference centers), but must also allow those who are addressed to share in determining the content of the kerygma. Form and content are not to be separated, because only in genuine communication with the other person can there be proclamation at all. We must take a radical departure from a one-way flow of traffic, and we must take seriously secularization, the world's becoming worldly, and in conversation with the worldlings (and with the worldling within ourselves) must make our appeal to the worldling, in Christ.

It is regrettable that de Graaf's article, although it was delivered as a lecture at the well-attended meeting of ministers of the Dutch Reformed Church in 1958, has had so little effect. If we take his position seriously that *no* kerygma is possible without communication and that communication assumes a taking seriously of secularized man (who lives even in the Christian!), then we must come to a radical renewal in theological and practical church activity. The communication theme is further treated in skillful and penetrating fashion in Eugene Nida's *Message and Mission,* which bears the subtitle ''The Communication of the Christian Faith.'' [5] The author is secretary of the American Bible Society,

21

38045

and he approaches the problem as a cultural anthropologist, linguist, and Bible translator. He illustrates it with an abundance of examples in the realm of Bible translating (especially into so-called primitive languages with limited possibilities of expression, but in any case possibilities that are utterly different from those in Hebrew and Greek) and in the realm of differences in cultural patterns; he gives evidence of possessing a pure theological perspective. I should like to bring out a couple of the main ideas of the book because they are of importance in our situation.

In his tenth chapter, "The Theological Basis of Communication," Nida speaks, among other things, of God's communication with man. Authentic communication implies even for God a total entering into human language and human living conditions. "This can only be done by a radical adjustment and the employment of the grid of human experience in a particular culture at a particular time." [6] Revelation thus assumes a self-limitation on God's part. This holds true even for God's revelation in Jesus Christ whose divinity we may not exalt by blurring his humanity. "In fact, in our desire to emphasize the deity of Jesus Christ, we must not destroy his humanity, or we make his life only a drama in which all the lines were memorized in advance. Similarly, to regard him only as human is to destroy completely the meaning of God's revelation of himself." [7] The absolute God ventures to stand constantly in relationship. The historically conditioned elements in his message do not serve as wrappings for a supratemporal truth, so that we must look through them in order to discover God's essential intention. Only in a historical and conditioned way can God seek fellowship with man, and he can confront him with the truth only when this truth is expressed in human language. In his proclamation God takes his human partner utterly seriously; his revelation takes place in the form of a dialogue. Hence we can never from our side speak objectively about revelation, about God. Moreover, says Nida, the divine communication

is essentially incarnational. Words in and of themselves are empty
if they are not translated into life, unless they take form in life.
This is true of Jesus, who was fully a man among men and in just
this way revealed God's intention for men. This applies also to the
Christian. "This same fundamental principle has been followed
throughout the history of the church, for God has constantly
chosen to use not only words but human beings as well to witness
to His grace; not only the message, but the messenger, not only
the Bible, but the Church."[8]

Thus God has chosen the limitations of human language and
human culture to reveal himself to man. In what man has done
with the message, the human limitations become even more
evident. "Nevertheless, it was the plan and purpose of God that
the message be committed to men, not proclaimed by angels."[9]
With all due respect, it is thanks to the Holy Spirit, the power with
which God works in human hearts, that in spite of all the human
limitations something nevertheless has come out well from the
divine communication. The process of communication, in which
we share, is a divine matter, not only because God has sought the
communication and imparts his truth, but also because God's
Spirit makes the message of fellowship alive in human hearts and
causes it to be propagated through limited human words and
deeds. Thus far Nida, whose argument joins directly with that of
de Graaf (though of course without his knowing it). The consequences of this point of departure for Bible translation and mis-
sions, and above all for conversation between church and world,
between believer and nonbeliever, are evident and are then also
fully worked out in Nida's book. But before we begin to focus
what is said here on our own situation, it is desirable, I believe, to
add some further points with reference to the theme of communication and to work them out in more detail. We can best treat this
if we begin with some data from the New Testament about Jesus'
communication with men.

Jesus' Communication with Men

In the first place it is necessary to underscore the point that Jesus was so completely man that many could continue in the opinion that he was an ordinary man. Objective proofs of his special relationship with God, his special power, his superhuman wisdom, in short, of his deity, are not given and furthermore cannot be given. If one should wish to point to the so-called miracles and to the greatest of these miracles, the resurrection, then it needs to be noted that the miracle becomes a sign only for faith. Miracle was indeed something special for Jesus' contemporaries, but it did not necessarily indicate a unique relationship between miracle-worker and God. In a sphere where the separation between the natural and the supernatural, in which our thinking more often than not is by nature entangled, did not exist, where people were much more readily open to the idea of divine intervention than we are, and where they regarded this as an ordinary thing, miracles could hardly function as proof of a fundamentally distinctive position for Jesus of Nazareth, of whom these were told. The distinction between miracle and sign is very fittingly indicated in John 6, when in a lengthy discourse Jesus gives an explanation to the miraculous feeding. He says then (vs. 26) to the Jews: "Truly, truly, I tell you, you seek me, not because you have seen signs, but because you have eaten of the loaves and are filled." These people do not believe, even though they have seen him (vs. 36). In order truly to see, one must believe, and belief is a gift of God: "No one can come to me unless the Father who sent me should draw him" (vs. 44). The sign functions only within the context of revelation and faith; interpretation of the sign assumes the presence of the Lord himself or of the Holy Spirit that is sent after him. The Spirit of Truth will point the way to the full truth (John 16:13).

These directions are indispensable not only for a good understanding of the extraordinary deeds which Jesus did, but also for an understanding of his ordinary actions. That is to say, it is not a matter of the strange or the ordinary, but of this man himself, who comes as a sign from God into the midst of men. For the sign in which all signs find their fulfillment, in principle the same holds true as for the others. Even for those who knew Jesus, the report of his resurrection was not at once believable, and they too needed a fuller exposition; the interpretation of the event, including God's saving intention, was what gave meaning to this event, not as an exception to the rule but as a sign of God's continuing redemptive involvement with mankind. The meaning of the message of the resurrection lies in the words, "I am with you always, even to the end of the world" (Matt. 28:20), in the communication which is not ended by death and cannot be broken by the powers of darkness. Even with respect to the resurrection, the event itself, the report of what happened and the interpretation of it, the proclamation and the belief in the proclamation form a unity in which we can indeed distinguish the components but can never separate them. Communication of and communication between, human communication and God's communication with us form an indissoluble unity.

In the second place: If Jesus' being and activity are closely bound up with his message and the message about him, can we then distinguish in this message some characteristic features which can provide guidelines for our proclamation to and our conversation with the world? Some main lines can be drawn here:

1. Nida rightly places great emphasis on the point that Jesus used ordinary human words because it was his intention to be understood. Now it is however always true that a word signifies something only in a particular context; it only begins to say what it has to say in the context of a particular sentence, spoken by a particular person in a particular situation. Nida also says this expressly, when he speaks of the incarnational aspect of God's

25

revelation. Thus a word always has an additional value that is personal; the true intention of it is made evident in a gesture, a look, an attitude. In the New Testament it is said of many that they came to believe after a single word, a single deed of Jesus. Here it becomes evident that faith not only has the significance of "becoming acquainted and knowing," but above all of trusting, acknowledging, and that under certain circumstances the part played by the transmission of information in the communication between Jesus (or God) and man can be slight.

2. In manner of life and preaching Jesus associates himself with those of his own time and nation, his neighbors. For example, he employs parables in his instruction. Insiders know how much has been written about the aim of the parables, and what a large role in this is played by the interpretation of Mark 4:11, 12. At the risk of appearing superficial, I wish to emphasize only one point in Jesus' use of the parables. A parable is an expanded simile, and it is customary to say of such figures that they must not be made to go on all fours. Yet we cannot dispense with them, because a comparison (both at the points where it applies and at the point where it no longer serves) has an illuminating effect. Agreement and contrast are both essential for the functioning of the comparison. Thus it is also with the parables of Jesus, which intend to make it clear to us how God acts for and deals with men and what the relationship of man with God ought to be. Reference then is constantly made to the agreement with "everyday life": "It is as with the case of . . ." Often, however, there also comes a point at which the listener must think, "That is strange; I had never thought of that." The parable of the lost son in Luke 15 finds its climax in the unusual forgiving attitude of the father and his reception of the son. On this point there is a contrast between the behavior of this father and that of many, though not all, fathers of Jesus' day. Jesus shows most clearly what he wishes to say by means of this contrast, but this contrast is contrast only thanks to

the fact that there are so many points of agreement. And it certainly is not true that the good news can only make use of the contrast and not of the agreement! In the parable of the unjust judge in Luke 18 we are admonished to persist in prayer, even if we think we are not being heard. The example then is given of a widow who finally gets justice from an unjust judge, by her pleading so long that it began to annoy this man. There is a clear agreement between the attitude which is asked of the believer and that which the woman displayed. The contrast consists in the fact that the woman actually had no right to hope to be heard and that the believer may trust that he will indeed be heard. If the unjust judge acted thus, Jesus says, "shall not God avenge his chosen ones who cry to him day and night?" (Luke 18:7).

3. What Jesus says and does is seen as the fulfilling of what was promised to the "fathers." There is a certain continuity between past and present. The message comes in the first place to the nation of Israel which stands in a peculiar relation to God: in order to understand what Jesus means, one must see his behavior in the light of what God has previously said to Israel and done for Israel. Yet immediately after the saying that not one jot or tittle of the law shall pass away (Matt. 5:18), there stands a series of utterances beginning with "you have heard that it was said of old" and ending with "but I say to you." Precisely because Jesus stands in a unique relation to God, to him is given the power to transcend law and tradition or to interpret them in a highly individual way. Here also it holds true that the message is proclaimed in a duality of agreement and contrast. "And all were greatly astonished, so that they asked each other, 'What is this? A new teaching with authority!' " (Mark 1:27). The proof from Scripture, the illustration and interpretation of Jesus' being and works with the help of utterances from the law, the prophets, and the writings (our Old Testament), played, as appears from the writings of the New Testament, a large role in the first Christians' reflection on their

27

faith. Recent studies have shown that in this process these Christians made use of methods which were also used by others. Much of what seems to us labored and foreign is not at all strange when it is compared with the use of Scripture by others. Yet there remains in this use of Scripture an element of personal choice, because here the issue is an explanation of this Jesus and his work. In the choice of these prooftexts, in the neglect of certain others, in the grouping of the utterances, in the lifting out of context and quoting in a different way, and so forth, it appears that not only does the Scripture make it clear how one is to regard Jesus, but also that only from the encounter with Jesus and belief in him does it become clear what the Scripture really intended.

The force of proof of the Scripture passages holds fully true only within the community. Outsiders can come under the impression of the force of arguments, of the inventiveness in the application of certain words; only when the crucial step is taken, when one gives his trust to Jesus, is this use of these Scripture passages also convincing.

4. Jesus' being and works are explained in the New Testament with the help of a great number of titles. I leave aside the question of which of these designations were used by Jesus himself and which were deemed suitable for application to him only by the first community. I state only that many and varied titles are used: Prophet, High Priest, Messiah, Son of Man, Lord, Savior, Son of God, the Word, and so on. In addition, still other designations also appear, such as the shepherd, the vine, the way, the truth, the life, and many others. When we investigate what is intended by these designations, we always find that on the one hand they can only be understood when one makes a thorough study of the use of these terms in the surrounding world of that time, and on the other hand, it appears again and again that they can be used only in a very special sense to indicate Jesus' relation to men and to God. Here too there are almost as many points of

contrast as of agreement, and those who come into contact with Jesus are constantly being asked to revise the notions which they bring with them from without. We use the title Christ almost automatically as a designation for Jesus and in so doing forget that his messiahship (messiah is the same as Christ) was anything but evident to his contemporaries. Anyone who confessed "Jesus is the Christ" had to lay emphasis upon the Christ as well as upon the Jesus in his confession. In a recent article, "Jesus the Christ," [10] W. C. van Unnik has said: "Now the trouble here is that the image of Jesus in the N. T., both in his earthly life and in his exalted state, has not very much in common with the picture of the Messianic King in Jewish sources. So the differences are usually underscored." But, he says, if the Christians' conception of the Messiah was totally different from that of others, how then did they come to call their Lord by this name? Van Unnik's article is concerned primarily then with the answer to the question of what points of agreement there were in spite of the sharp contrast. It is always true that the contrast makes sense only if there is also agreement!

Characteristic thus of the proclamation of and about Jesus in the New Testament is always the use of the language, the concepts, the images, the theology of the environment. Without this use no communication was possible; but it is always true that the language, the concepts, and so forth, can be used only up to a certain point. The distinctive thing about what must be said, the unique quality of this man in his relation to God and to men makes it necessary that the concepts and images used be shattered, that they be accepted *and* rejected in their limitations, and that they are serviceable for the proclamation only if recoined. It is always a matter of a paraphrase, of a hedging about with human words of a reality which in principle and in fact again and again breaks through the hedge and rises above it. Yet the hedge is sensible, because, thanks to this paraphrase, it becomes clear where we must seek and shall find and at what points the paraphrase must prove inadequate.

The Variety in the New Testament Witness

Variety is a highly characteristic mark of the New Testament proclamation. This mark is directly related to what was said in the foregoing section. One paraphrase or description is not adequate. The proclamation comes to man with the aid of various descriptions, all of which in turn are inadequate at another point. Jesus is Messiah *and* high priest *and* Lord *and* Word. There is not one comparison; there are many. There is not one prooftext or a standard set of texts; in all sorts of ways and in very different ways, the connection is established between Jesus' appearance and speaking and that which is testified to about God's concern with Israel and the world, a testimony that is borne in the Scriptures. In this process there is also room for the personal viewpoint of the preacher or of the group that is making the proclamation. There are obvious differences between Mark, Matthew, Luke, John, Paul, and James. They do not say the same thing, even though they begin with the unique significance of the same person and intend to bear witness to him. The data available to these writers came to them by way of particular men and groups in various circumstances, and for this reason their proclamation is varied. What is fascinating about the study of the New Testament lies precisely in the tracing out and describing in detail of the kaleidoscopic and variegated diversity of the witness. Why does this author now say just this and not that? What must his hearers and readers have thought of this? Where now is to be found the commonality that he allows to stand, and where do we detect the wholly different?

In this it is evident that people had no inclination to make a choice, but thought rather in terms of complement. It is rarely an

either-or, but almost always a both-and. One must only note the
diversity of scriptural data which Paul uses in order to make clear
the divine intention in Jesus' suffering and death! The Pauline
doctrine of atonement is much more varied and richer than the
traditional Reformation doctrine which likes to call itself Pauline.
And one must only note the multiplicity of images which are used
in the New Testament to denote the church. Paul Minear, in his
splendid book, *Images of the Church in the New Testament,* [11]
counts no fewer than ninety-six! There, the author notes these
images are often interwoven; they complement and correct each
other (a splendid example of this is Eph. 2:11-22). Of this Minear
says, "The metaphors themselves are secondary deductions from
the primal communal experience. This may result, as we have
seen, in a profuse mixing of metaphors, but the mixture itself
reflects not logical confusion but theological vitality." Then he
quotes K. Stendahl, who in another connection remarks, "Over
against stringent logic (the way of thinking of later theology)
stands Jewish thinking in images, where contradictory facts and
conceptions can be put together in a kind of significant
mosaic." [12] Minear has previously made it clear that the images
do not encompass the reality to which they refer, let alone coincide with it. "The reality has too much height and depth to permit
verbal idolatry of that sort." [13] Indeed, even the church is not a
reality in itself, but is always connected with the Lord and the
Spirit. One of the means, we can add, of combatting the verbal
idolatry is the very multiplicity of concepts and images with
which God's work in the world is described.

The Conversation Within the Church
and the Conversation Between Church and World

We return to our point of departure. The foregoing underscores
the correctness of the thesis that the conversation within the

church about the central points of the faith must be coupled with a maximal openness to the problems of modern times.

The church will be able really to make her proclamation only when she does this in the words, concepts, and images of her own time. This holds true not only for the proclamation to the outsiders, but also quite certainly for the reflection on the faith of her own members, who are modern men and must also be such to the full if they do not mean to shut themselves up in a Christian ghetto. One needs only to read the report of the SCM conference which A. W. Cramer gave in the November, 1962, issue of *Wending*[14] to realize how much the worldly way of thinking is also the way of thinking of the Christians. Church and world are not two entities set over against each other. We cannot keep secularization at arm's length (and out of our minds), but we must accept the fact that the secularized world is a part of our own being. But must the Christian not be converted? Yes, of course. Must he not proclaim that which transcends this world? Yes, of course. But he can only do this (and the church can only do this) if he begins at the beginning. If we do not think and live entirely as men of our own time, we shall never be able to bring about the communication to which we ought to contribute in the service of Jesus Christ, nor shall we ever be able to find a genuine answer to our own questions. I quote Dr. Cramer: "How do you convince the ungodly when you acknowledge his own questions and yet understand that your answers do not satisfy him and you have no other answers available? Connected with this is a third point: people began then to wonder what the story is with their own faith and with the way in which the Bible functions in their own faith. This self-examination of the believer was a much more radical matter than the originally anticipated investigation into the possible renewal in the communication of the gospel'' (p. 584).

The conversation within the church is an antiquated, irrelevant thing if it is not directly related to the conversation between church and world. The conversation between the various types of belief and between the churches must not deal with the controversial points of the past, but must concern itself with the problems of the present. If we take this task seriously, it will appear that we can leave behind us a great heap of ballast of the centuries. The study of the intellectual strife of earlier centuries, and especially of the past century, is fruitful for thinking through the task of the church in the present only insofar as one can show at what points people shared in the use of the thought categories of that time and at what points they said no and thereby acted for the sake of the gospel of the Lord who transcends and goes beyond all thought categories. And in so doing one then also gives critical consideration to the question of where people went too far in sharing the thought of the times, and where they too quickly or improperly set themselves in opposition to the spirit of the times. In the evaluation of the past the opinions will often diverge, and the opinions will often be determined in part by a connection with certain figures and currents in that past. This is not wrong, provided that in our conversation we only take care that we conduct it *now,* and that the decisions made *then* cannot merely be parroted. What is needed (according to the "Theses for Conversation Between Different Church Parties," already cited above) is "a maximal openness to the questions of a scientific, social, and human sort, with which we shall be confronted in increasing measure by the 'atomic age' that has dawned." The questions of the world are the questions of the church, because the members of the church live entirely in the world. Necessary also is a concentration on the person and work of Christ, and confidence in the Holy Spirit. Concentration on the person and work of Christ can never be the same as repeating the New Testament witness about him in words that are somehow adapted to the present time. Translating is more than transposing. Translating presupposes a total immersion in the *other* idiom. A few footnotes at the bottom of the page and some

33

explanations of classical dogma are not only inadequate; they mistake the essential problem. We cannot simply repeat John the Baptist's confession, "Behold the Lamb of God that takes away the sin of the world" (John 1:29), and proclaim this as the heart of the Christian confession for all times, let alone use it to measure anyone's orthodoxy. That is to say, this confession functions only in a particular context, in which the terms "Lamb of God," "world," and "takes away sin" are meaningful. Now assuming that we could determine why John said just this, what he meant by it, and in what context he spoke this word (which does not appear to be exactly an easy matter; was John thinking of the passover lamb? or of Isaiah 53? or of a sacrificial lamb?), we still cannot stop with this explanation. As men of the present time we shall have to try to determine how we shall describe with different words, in a different intellectual, cultural, and social context, what was written nineteen hundred years ago with the expression "Lamb of God that takes away the sin of the world." In so doing we shall discover that this is extremely difficult, that various solutions are possible, and that communication with the man of today has an influence not only formally but also materially upon the church's proclamation. (And then in the formula just quoted we still have treated only one facet of the rich New Testament witness!) When, on the other hand, someone says in all sincerity, "I do not believe that Jesus is the Lamb of God that takes away the sin of the world," then we may not, solely on the basis of this statement, brand him as an unbeliever or a heretic. Then we shall have to ask *what* makes belief impossible for him: the obvious "transposing" of an ancient statement into the present and the use of this statement as an adequate formulation of contemporary faith, *or* even that which was described in the original context. Then it is precisely *with* this man, who so strongly experiences the difference between the twentieth century and the first century that the first-century formulation becomes meaningless to him, that a

34

search must be made for a confession that arises out of a concentration on the nature and work of the Lord, and that at the same time intends to be fully contemporary. Therein conversion is an absolute demand, not only in the case of this unbeliever or heretic, but also for those who have less difficulty with the biblical expression: a conversion to the Lord, which also presupposes the readiness at a given moment to say an unequivocal no to all that is modern, natural, and acceptable in the present time and thus to provide a place in the confession for the contrast. But also a conversion to the world, a renunciation of all verbal idolatry (even when it involves biblical words), a thinking together with the thought of one's own time, a sharing in the life of one's own time. The distressing thing about the discussion that goes on in the church is often the fact that the conservatives are ready with their condemnation of the progressives because, in the opinion of the former, the latter by sharing in the thinking of their own time neglect essential points of the gospel, and the fact that the conservatives do not realize that through their not being radical enough, they fall just as far short in their mission. Conversely, the progressives often opt for a confrontation with their own time in such a way that they fail to discern that standing in the breach for the old can also go hand in hand with a clinging to what is essential. To preach in communication with one's own time is to advance along a narrow path, between chasms, led and held fast by the Holy Spirit, without whom no genuine communication is possible. We cannot secure insurance against losing our footing, and it certainly is better to accept the risk of slipping than to yield to the mood of caution.

Concluding Remarks

In the foregoing, all the emphasis is placed on the main point, the connection between the conversation within the church and

35

that with the man outside the church. Now following that it is proper and worthwhile in conclusion to touch on some points which are related to this theme.

1. Where do we stand with respect to the figurative way of speaking in the Bible? And can we still think in complementary fashion? Or are we, both inside and outside the church, too much occupied with analyzing? We shall have to accept the fact that various images, expressions, and methods of approach tumble over each other, supplement each other, or are even logically contradictory. Perhaps the theologians, before they begin to conduct the conversation with the man outside the church and their conversations with each other, will first have to be apprenticed to the poets!

2. We shall have to take seriously what Nida calls the incarnational aspect. We debate about reconciliation, and sometimes the debate gets hot and heavy. When Paul writes in II Cor. 5:13-21 about reconciliation, he does so out of a new, reconciled life: "And he died for all, that those who live should no longer live for themselves but for him who died for them." Our talking is not only unconvincing and untrue, but also beside the point if our life, personal and corporate, is not a life rooted in reconciliation.

3. After what has been said, one could have the feeling that now nothing is any longer fixed: that the space in which we believe and bear witness is so broad and that the intellectual flexibility that is demanded is so great that the boundaries of church and world become blurred and the question of truth in fact can no longer be considered. Are there indeed, in the last analysis, any boundaries? Can there indeed come a moment when we must say that the other person has gone off the narrow path, has abandoned the essential content of the message for the sake of the new forms?

In his article mentioned above, de Graaf says: "Communication signifies holding to the truth, growing up into him who is the head, Christ. The church must maintain this truth to which we cling, but this same church must grow, in communication. *Excommunication assumes a level of communication and catholicity that we are far from having reached, if indeed we shall ever reach it''* (p. 215). One can remark that this does not provide an answer to the question posed above, but *can* we give an answer? Eph. 4:11-16, the passage to which de Graaf alludes, speaks of the concentration on the center, on him who is the living center of the church, from whom all powers flow and to whom all ought to be directed. Paul obviously thinks that if this concentration is present "all sorts of winds of doctrine" and "the cunning craftiness of men" will have no chance or at least can be recognized and rejected. Even on the matter of discipline Jesus' saying ought to apply: "Seek ye first his kingdom and his righteousness and all this will be given to you as well" (Matt. 6:33 RSV).

III

The Inquiry
After the Man
Jesus of Nazareth

Introduction

The historical investigation into the life of Jesus—usually identified by the German term *Leben-Jesu-Forschung*—is one of the most fascinating chapters in theology.[1]

In this chapter I propose to undertake to show nonspecialists *how* fascinating it is, and *why* it is fascinating. Precisely in the present time, when in the life of faith of many the emphasis is being placed on the human side of Jesus, and for many he means more as the true man, the one who shows us what being human really implies, than as the Son of God, it is worthwhile to examine how we can encounter this man as his contemporaries encountered him. Gerhard Ebeling has said that our times are more interested in concrete persons and events than in eternal truths. The true humanity of Jesus (to use the terminology of the ancient dogma) is no longer a problem, though his true deity is. Can we however approach this man historically without involving God in the discussions, and if we make a place for God, are we then still actually engaged in historical investigation?

Albert Schweitzer

In his famous book of 1913, *Geschichte der Leben-Jesu-Forschung* (ET, "The Quest of the Historical Jesus"), Albert Schweitzer has given a survey of the study of the life of Jesus, primarily in Germany. He begins with an anonymous writing published by Lessing in 1778, *Von dem Zwecke Jesu und seiner Jünger* (ET, "The Goal of Jesus and His Disciples"). This was the work of Reimarus, a scholar from the time of the Enlightenment, who for the first time in history attempted, with the aid of historical methods, to separate the preaching of Jesus from the witness of the Christians concerning him. Reimarus' approach is typical of the Leben-Jesu-Forschung in the entire period from about 1780 to 1910 which Schweitzer is describing. People strove to go behind the ecclesiastical and dogmatic theories (even behind the testimony of Jesus' first disciples in the New Testament) concerning the Christ of faith back to the Jesus of history. They expected that without the many fabrications woven about him by pious Christians, the prophet of Nazareth in his simplicity would shine forth all the more clearly and would be able to be a guide for modern men in an entirely different way from that of the preceding eighteen centuries. In this they not only went against what had been regarded by the church's tradition as sacred and untouchable, but often also were obliged to proceed against their own positions. "The critical study of the life of Jesus has been for theology a school of honesty," says Schweitzer.[2] Stumbling and getting up again, ever anew experimenting, people tried to give a historical sketch of Jesus of Nazareth which could satisfy both mind and heart.

The results of this experimenting are subjected to thoroughgoing criticism by Schweitzer. People have assimilated Jesus to themselves too much and have unjustly modernized him; they have also unconsciously recognized as genuine that which fitted in with their own convictions and rejected what was foreign and did not fit in, calling it later tradition.

There was a danger that we should offer them a Jesus who was too small, because we had forced Him into conformity with our human standards

39

and human psychology. To see that, one need only read the Lives of Jesus written since the sixties, and notice what they have made of the great imperious sayings of the Lord, how they have weakened down His imperative world-contemning demands upon individuals, that He might not come into conflict with our ethical ideals, and might tune His denial of the world to our acceptance of it. Many of the greatest sayings are found lying in a corner like explosive shells from which the charges have been removed.

The study of the Life of Jesus has had a curious history. It set out in quest of the historical Jesus, believing that when it had found Him it could bring Him straight into our time as a Teacher and Saviour. It loosed the bands by which He had been riveted for centuries to the stony rocks of ecclesiastical doctrine, and rejoiced to see life and movement coming into the figure once more, and the historical Jesus advancing, as it seemed, to meet it. But He does not stay; He passes by our time and returns to His own.[3]

Schweitzer himself pictures Jesus as a child of his own time, and indeed as an apocalypticist who expects the end of time at any moment and for this conviction devotes everything and offers his life. This Jesus is a strange figure, motivated by ideas which cannot be ours. It is also an oversimplification to think that he himself should have proclaimed eternal truths and religious and ethical ideas valid for all ages, while the antiquated dogmatic conceptions should have descended from his disciples. Jesus too let himself be led by a dogmatics and in so doing did not ask whether this dogmatics fitted into our modern world.

What can we as believers do with such an alien Jesus? As thoroughgoing as his portrayal of Jesus as a man who is firmly set in the conceptual world of his time is Schweitzer's declaration that we are not bound to these conceptions (in the matter of the anticipation of an imminent end of the world). It is not the conception but the will that is important. ''Our relation to the historical Jesus must be honest and free. We concede to history its

40

right and free ourselves from his conceptual material. But we bow before the mighty will that stands behind this and seek to serve him in our time, that in our wills he may be born to new life and work and may work at our perfection and the world's. In this we find the being-at-one with the infinite moral world-will and become children of the kingdom of God."[4]

Schweitzer's analysis of the Leben-Jesu-Forschung had both a revelatory and a disheartening effect. In the years following 1913 only a few have ventured to write a biography of Jesus. Only in our time have people actually begun to engage themselves intensively with the questions about Jesus' life, though this in a way totally different from that of the liberal Leben-Jesu-Forschung of the nineteenth century or even from that of Schweitzer.

Schweitzer—I do not propose here to deal further with the historical merits of his picture of the apocalypticist Jesus—still had recognized the possibility and the rightness of the effort to come, through historical critical investigation of the sources, to a reconstruction of the life of Jesus. His own reconstruction rests primarily on a combination of the data found in Mark and Matthew. After World War I, however, some not only denied, on historical grounds, the possibility of such a reconstruction, but also, on dogmatic grounds, the propriety of the effort as such. The former denial came chiefly from the side of the so-called form-critical school and the latter chiefly from the side of Karl Barth and his disciples.

The Gospels as
Sources of Early Christian Tradition

After 1918, many scholars (of whom Rudolf Bultmann, Martin Dibelius, and Karl Ludwig Schmidt have become the most famous) occupied themselves with the form in which the gospel narratives (especially in the first three gospels) have come down to us. It was discovered that we actually have only loose stories and sayings which after a period of oral transmission were fixed in writing in various ways and united in the three gospels. Typical anecdotes, striking debates, pieces of catechetical material concerning Jesus, a longer connecting piece of passion narrative, stereotyped miracle stories, detached, easily memorized aphorisms—an abundance of material was ready at hand for the gospel writers. They have selected it and placed it in a certain framework, and in so doing they undoubtedly intend to provide a responsible idea of matters; yet either consciously or unconsciously they allowed themselves to be guided by the questions and needs of the communities for which they wrote. And what holds true for the evangelists in the period from *ca.* 65 to 85 of course also holds true for the oral tradition and the written sources which they used. In the period from *ca.* 30 to 65 also there was much that happened and much that changed. The first Christians were not psychologically or historically interested in Jesus of Nazareth after the fashion of a professor of the nineteenth or twentieth century, but they were testifying about their Lord. Anyone who seeks the historical Jesus ultimately comes face to face with the early Christian kerygma, the proclamation of the community. The preaching is anything but uniform; there is a great variety in form and content, and it is very difficult, if not impossible, to distinguish here between what is usable for us as a source for the life of Jesus and what is nothing but *Gemeindetheologie* (i.e., the theology of the community).

Of course people have made the attempt to find criteria which they could use. The investigation of the forms is at the same time an investigation of the tradition and of the *Sitz im Leben,* that is to say, the situation out of which one can explain a particular story. That a particular incident or a particular saying was handed down and that this happened in a particular way (sometimes in different ways in different gospels) must be explained in terms of the situation of the community or communities which handed down this saying. By means of comparison between the different versions of a story one can frequently show that it has been adapted to a new formulation of the problem, one that was not yet current in the time of Jesus himself. Through an analysis of the tradition one can thus attempt to separate the original from what was added later, the authentic from the inauthentic. In so doing it appeared easier in practice to hold something to be inauthentic than to demonstrate that a particular datum belongs to the very earliest stratum of tradition. Bultmann distinguishes the proclamation of Hellenistic Christianity, that of the earliest Aramaic-speaking Christian community, and the words of Jesus himself. All that can be explained out of the situation, belonging to the first-named stages of the tradition, is a dubious datum for the reconstruction of Jesus' life. Actually we can make use only of the data which cannot be explained from and in terms of earliest Christianity or from Judaism, and these data are not numerous. In his little book entitled *Jesus* (1926; ET, "Jesus and the Word," 1931), Bultmann then also says: "I do indeed think that we can now know almost nothing concerning the life and personality of Jesus, since the early Christian sources show no interest in either, are moreover fragmentary and often legendary; and other sources about Jesus do not exist." [5] As a believer Bultmann also draws from this some radical conclusions for dogmatics, as will be set forth presently.

Dogmatic Objections

Of course the liberal representatives of the Leben-Jesu-Forschung in the nineteenth century had also had their conservative opponents. These latter tried to save what there was to save in this iconoclastic wave, denied that one could measure Jesus by ordinary human measures, and assumed that this man had special powers at his disposal and thereby had been able to perform all sorts of miracles. People were indeed prepared to concede that on all sorts of details uncertainty could prevail, but ultimately it was thought one could with good conscience connect the titles and utterances of traditional dogmatics with this great figure. However, according to Karl Barth in his chapter on David Friedrich Strauss in his *Die protestantische Theologie im 19. Jahrhundert* (ET "Protestant Theology in the Nineteenth Century"),[6] liberals and conservatives had more in common than they thought. They all thought that somewhere in history they could find a concrete handle for their faith to grasp. As an ideal man or as Son of God, Jesus is a historically understandable personality upon whom faith can build. Over against this Karl Barth places a radically different view; he will have no more of such a historicizing or psychologizing of Jesus Christ than of a religious consciousness in man that is tuned to God's revelation. In matters of faith and revelation there is nothing to localize and grasp; one can only be addressed and believe. Barth praises the radical D. F. Strauss because the latter, in his first *Leben Jesu* of 1835-36, at that time notorious, demonstrated that the reconstruction of a picture of Jesus was an impossible undertaking. Barth then formulates the problem himself as follows:[7] (a) Does not the connecting of the faith with particular events within history signify a denial of the nature of faith? (b) Our sources are meant all the way through to be testimony. (c) If we wish to discover a historical figure behind these sources, we can find this figure only by leaving aside all that is essential for the witnessing. What remains then has nothing to do with the faith of the apostles. (d) The historical Jesus is at most a relatively great person and in no case "the incarnate Word, fulfilling God's decision with respect to us and calling us to decision." Historical scholarship cannot say to us who Jesus actually was; only faith which yields to the proclamation that comes to us in the gospel can hear what is

44

essential. Faith cannot be prepared for or supported by means of reasoning or investigation; seen from man's side it is a leap, and from God's side a gift. Later on Barth came to think more affirmatively about the relation of revelation and history; in the twenties and thirties, however, it was a settled thing for him that the Leben-Jesu-Forschung was not only in practice but in principle a fruitless and disastrous undertaking.

In many respects Bultmann was and is in agreement with this view of Barth's. In the introduction to his *Jesus and the Word* he says that it is not the task of the historian objectively and dispassionately to analyze a bit of history, but it is to allow himself to be addressed by history in continuing dialogue. "Encounter with history" becomes the key term. An existentialist view of history demands of the historian that he dare to place himself in the balances, and the proclamation as it comes to us in the gospel sources demands faith from the hearer. Anyone who wishes to write down in a chronicle how it actually was gets no further than a summing-up of facts; he cannot trace out what historically was genuinely important, what continued to have its impact and has *made* history. Anyone who wishes to collect the facts, major and minor, about Jesus not only gets his hands on precious little, but also certainly will not find what he is looking for. For the believer, Jesus' life and personality are completely immaterial, but his proclamation, which can be rediscovered with difficulty by means of analysis of the various strata of tradition, continues to speak to us; whenever we let ourselves be taught by it and venture to reinterpret this into terms of our own time, we have done what we as historians and as believers ought to do.

Down to his latest publications Bultmann has held firm to this line. He repeatedly emphasizes that the proclamation will not let itself be legitimated by particular facts. Thus in 1960 he still says: "The combination of historical report and kerygmatic christology in the Synoptic Gospels is not for the purpose of giving

45

legitimacy to the Christ-kerygma, but quite the reverse, of giving legitimacy to the history of Jesus as messianic history, as it were, by viewing it in the light of kerygmatic christology, to legitimate Jesus' history, so to speak, as messianic history.'' [8] Briefly put, it is not history that proves the kerygma, but the kerygma that discloses the meaning of the history.

Efforts at Breaking the Impasse

Historical Arguments

For a long time the Leben-Jesu-Forschung, and the resistance to it as well, were a German province. Most of the English New Testament scholars up until very recently have shown themselves skeptical toward the working methods of the form-critical school, and they have been able to arouse little or no attention or comprehension for the systematic considerations of Barth and Bultmann and others.[9] The American scholar J. M. Robinson has reproached the English and the French for having actually continued, on a modest scale and avoiding the extremes, the German Forschung of the nineteenth century.[10] The reproach is justly made; yet this more sober investigation has led to a better understanding of the limitations of the form-critical methods. It is admitted that in the entire New Testament, interpretation and factual recitation are intertwined, and therewith full account is taken of the study of the sources. Inquiry into the *Sitz im Leben* of the material handed down to us is legitimate—but in addition to the *Sitz im Leben* in the early church we must also inquire into the possible *Sitz* in the life of Jesus. The Gospels after all do not purport to give the history of the Christian community, but to be books about Jesus of Nazareth! Interpretation and the handing on of particular facts then may not be separated; in our analysis we must not place so much emphasis upon the proclaimed elements that we forget that the evangelists really do purport to describe all sorts of events out of the life of Jesus. The Gospel of John itself, which does so much "interpreting" that Schweitzer and Bultmann are not willing to draw any data from it, proclaims as the central truth that the Word of God has become flesh, has dwelt among us, and that we have beheld him in all his glory. The eyewitnesses have handed down the message of what they have seen, and all that the church says about Jesus and about God is based upon their testimony.

According to the form critics we have only small bits of tradition remaining, and it was only the evangelists who first placed these bits in a particular setting. But is it conceivable that people handed down these stories detached from each other and had no interest in historical connections? The passion narrative, with all the variations among the Gospels, still relates a clear succession of events. Why should the second generation have been interested, and not the first, in a well-arranged narrative about the development of events? Finally, the preaching of the first generation of Christians relied upon, and could be corrected by, eyewitnesses—both among friends and among opponents. These will not have applied historical-critical standards, but would certainly have intervened if, out of pious considerations, preachers had related inaccuracies about the Lord. In short: the tradition was more a reproduction than a production. Besides, we must not underestimate the capacity of Jesus' contemporaries for memorization (they had no stenographers' notebooks or memorandum books and thus were dependent on a trained memory).

Finally, we must also point out a deficiency in the form-critical method: in the comparison between the strata and forms of tradition one can indeed detect the differences and on this basis distinguish later and earlier elements, but one cannot determine to what extent people in later times properly handed down unaltered

47

all sorts of older motifs. We cannot trace what the Christian communities in various periods of the first century had in common with Jesus *and* the view which Jesus shared with his Palestinian contemporaries. The form critics live on minimum rations, while we in our own reflections must involve the maximum, the whole of the early Christian tradition which purports to tell about Jesus. From all sides this tradition points toward a center, and in that center stands the one about whom all is concerned.

Careful and tenacious investigation of the gospel reports, together with a study of the world in which Jesus lived (and about which we still are constantly acquiring new data), can actually help us better to understand Jesus and the earliest reports about him. In his book, *Wat weten wij van Jezus van Nazareth?*[11] ("What Do We Know of Jesus of Nazareth?"), A. F. J. Klijn has given a survey of the material at our disposal and has attempted to arrange this in comprehensible order.

The Developments Within the School of Bultmann

The many pupils of Bultmann[12] generally speaking hold to the form-critical criteria given by their teacher in their approach to the biblical material. They are prepared to work with the acknowledged minimum of established data and show that they are not impressed by the arguments listed in the foregoing section. Yet they come to other conclusions than did their teacher and regard the preaching and the attitude of Jesus himself as a central issue for historical and systematic theology.

In broad outline, their argument comes down to this: the first Christians did not intend to be giving a biography, but rather a proclamation concerning a Lord who, crucified and risen from the dead, demands of us repentance, faith, and obedience. But of this exalted Lord the proclaiming community says that he is the same as the man Jesus. They were not telling a myth about a heavenly being; they rejected any spiritualizing and blurring; they were telling a story about deeds and words of a man from Nazareth. We do not know precisely what this Jesus did and with what words he spoke about himself, but we do know that for his followers there existed a continuity between what their master had said and had claimed to be and what they were proclaiming about him. Jesus then may not have known and used the Christological titles and conceptions by which the later preaching sought to characterize his behavior and his preaching; he acted in such a way, with authority, that people began searching for utterly unique words and concepts in order to describe this unique man. In other words, in the words of Jesus which are held by Bultmann and company to be authentic, we find no explicit Christology—Jesus did not call himself Messiah, Son of Man, and so on—but we do find an implicit one. Jesus' words and deeds form a unity. We cannot write a biography; we can be in disagreement about the genuineness of various sayings. Of many narratives we cannot ascertain whether they go back to actual events, but still we know who Jesus was.

It is also of the greatest importance dogmatically for us as believers that there is a continuity between the preaching of Jesus and the preaching about him—in the first community and in the church of the present day. The kerygma then may not be interested in the man Jesus in our way; it speaks about him and claims to speak about him in a justifiable fashion. It is not a shot in the dark, not a fabrication. If the kerygma should consist in a number of assertions which in a more or less accidental and historically utterly unverifiable way are connected with a person Jesus who is chosen at random, then the kerygma would be no more than a myth; perhaps very profound and very true, but timelessly hovering above the world, above history, and above our concrete human existence as well. We shall never be able to prove the kerygma (as Bultmann says, we can never legitimate it), but the proclamation itself pushes us back to the question about

49

this one who is proclaimed and who has proclaimed himself. "The figure of Jesus," says Gerhard Ebeling, "does not appear in an arbitrary disguise in the christological kerygma, for the kerygma makes explicit that which was implicit in his person, i.e. in his appearance and preaching." [13] The kerygma calls us to a decision, to a leap—but not to a leap into the unknown. We do not ask for obedience to ourselves, and even the apostles did not claim any authority for themselves. They and we may and must tell in whose name the urgent summons to men is addressed and why this is properly done. This means that we must speak responsibly about Jesus in order to be able to bear witness trustworthily. And to speak responsibly means for us also always to speak a historical response.

Ebeling names three important points[14]: (1) Words can have different meanings; even the words used by Jesus are, taken in themselves, capable of more than one interpretation. Just because they have reference to Jesus, however, they have acquired a very particular connotation, and we can trace this out by asking who he was. (2) Only by starting out from Jesus has it been possible to proclaim the kerygma. Jesus is not only the object, the content of the proclamation, but also its foundation and source. (3) There is in the early Christian kerygma a multiplicity of formulations; in this multiplicity, what is cohesive and essential is the fact that all the formulations refer to Jesus.

In addition to Ebeling's criticism of Bultmann, reference should be made here to the approach made by E. Käsemann in some articles which are to be found in the volume *Exegetische Versuche und Besinnungen*[15] (ET, "New Testament Questions of Today"). In his *Sackgassen im Streit um den historischen Jesus* ("Blind Alleys in the Jesus of History Controversy"), he remarks with reference to his teacher Bultmann that it was not without reason that Bultmann's star witness, John, did clothe the kerygma in the form of a gospel. When one is not interested in the earthly

Jesus and concentrates one's attention entirely upon the exalted Lord, one does not write a gospel! Indeed, according to Käsemann, because in various parts of the early church enthusiastic preachers (in the literal sense of the word) appealed to the Spirit and the necessity of distinguishing the spirits became acute, people referred back to what the earthly Jesus had done and said.[16] "The real problem is not how to give faith a historical foundation; it is how to use the critical method to separate the true message from falsifications of it, and to do this we need the help of the very One who was at that very time the historical Jesus, not by accident but by divine necessity."[17]

This is still a long way from answering the question as to the trustworthiness of the various traditions in the historical critical sense. But it is important to note that in their testimony, their instruction in the faith, their defense of the faith, and their other speaking about God, people emphatically purported to be speaking about Jesus of Nazareth; that they thus knew themselves to be bound to particular essential events of the past and wished to interpret the meaning of what had happened then in the light of what they had experienced later (described as the resurrection of the Lord and his return to the Father, and the presence of the exalted Lord in the community), operative in the situation of the present.[18]

Some Conclusions

From the two preceding sections it is evident that the question of the man Jesus of Nazareth still is a very crucial question. We see the danger signs raised in warning by Schweitzer, Barth, and Bultmann, but we know that we must answer this question. We do not wish to and we must not retreat to a proclamation that comes vertically from above, to a timeless idea, or to an ecclesiastical authority that guarantees the trustworthiness of historically uncertain data. We cannot stop with a historical skepticism, because a message can have authority for us only if a tangible person stands behind it. It is good to be able to point to the attitude toward life of the first Christians and of many others after them, who have given form in tangible deeds to the message and the faith, but we should like to know that these people have not committed themselves to an illusion. For the sake of faith we need ever anew to seek after the man Jesus.

What ways then are open to us? I shall attempt cautiously to formulate some conclusions and thus to draw some lines along which the specialist and the ordinary Bible reader can make some further progress.

1. We have *only* the testimony of the first Christians. We must constantly keep in mind the character of proclamation that belongs to all our sources.

2. Our first obligation is to understand that testimony, to investigate how the words were used, and why they were used (and other terms were not used). This means study of the various facets of the testimony, the varied terminology, and comparison with extra-biblical usage of words: in short, the usual work of the exegete with the help of concordance, grammar, lexicon, and commentary, that the ordinary Bible reader will be able to follow, thanks to all the aids that are produced with him in mind.

3. Words and concepts point to living men who use them, not only to their ideas, but to their total being in the world. The authors of the New Testament writings and Jesus himself as children of their own time will appear different from ourselves, and we must not modernize them (Schweitzer). But they need not remain strangers to us. Ideas, truths of faith, and formulas only become compelling and convincing if we recognize or at least feel some human connection with the person(s) behind them.

4. We need to study the milieu (intellectual, political, economic) in which Jesus and his first followers lived. We must

52

especially also study the religious ideas of the time and then ask ourselves why and to what extent the Christians and Jesus himself thought differently and thus also acted differently from the Jewish and non-Jewish contemporaries. Of course we must also explore what they had in common with their surroundings. In this way we can trace out what is distinctive and even unique about Jesus and about the views of his followers.

5. In brief: we attempt to investigate what is the central point to which the various concepts refer and what these stories in their variety and multiplicity, written in different and even later situations, all are intending to tell us: in other words, what they mean to say about Jesus and why they mean to say this about him.

6. In this connection it will appear that these testimonies do not evoke one picture of the man Jesus, but illumine different facets of his human existence. In the fashion of the form-critical school we may make a distinction between earlier and later witnesses and obviously may take into account different intellectual and geographical situations in which particular stories have acquired their form. We shall have to sift them critically, but must keep in mind that even late witnesses, when they make explicit what is implicitly present, can be very valuable. Even this critical investigation is not able to point to one view of Jesus as the most nearly original one. From the first encounters between Jesus and men there have been different pictures of Jesus formed and corrected by means of these encounters with him and through conversations of people about him. Jesus rises above the testimonies of his followers; the historical Jesus will always be greater than the Jesus of the historians and the Jesus of the church.

7. Thus we must not try to harmonize by fitting everything into one large whole. We do unconsciously make a Jesus after our own image and likeness. A psychological approach is not the way to the goal. Nor is it any more possible or fruitful to write a biography of Jesus. The data in the various gospels cannot be

53

fitted together as pieces of a jigsaw puzzle. On certain main points we do get something of a historical handhold, namely in the passion narrative (see the book by Klijn mentioned above), and of course this helps us to understand various reactions of people and various ones of Jesus' words and deeds, but then it becomes even more evident to us that what is essential about him cannot be grasped.

8. What role does our belief (or our unbelief) play in this investigation? A historian can never be satisfied with merely recording the facts. He will also want to classify and explain them and try to show connections and developments. He will want to understand men from the past in their utterances and their actions. This can happen only in a subtle alternation of engagement and detachment, of sharing in life and viewing from a distance, in which the person of the historian is at stake.

It is not different with the investigation of the life of Jesus. The believing historian will, thanks to a certain congeniality, sometimes be able to see more keenly than the nonbeliever, but he will also note again and again how much he tends to assimilate Jesus to himself. His own insights of faith, whether traditional or modern, need constantly to be corrected. The nonbelieving historian will more easily take a detached position and thereby will be able in certain respects to make sounder judgments. He will note, however, that he cannot remain neutral but must take a stand; he can eventually discover that in his neutrality in fact he has already taken a stand, positively or negatively.

Historical research will never be able to prove the truth of the preaching of Christianity, and it will never be able to show that Jesus correctly claimed to have a special relation to God and that he thus rightly appeared with a special authority. Historical investigation also will never be able to deny this. Faith is a gift and in the last analysis needs no proof. But God can use historical investigation in order to prepare the way for the believing encounter between man and Jesus, between man and himself. And the Christian faith will, on its own account, constantly have to pose the question "Who was the man Jesus?" and will have also to attempt to give a historical and scientific answer to this question.

IV

Search for
a Modern
Christology

Introduction

This chapter is concerned with the fourth chapter of J. A. T. Robinson's famous book *Honest to God*. It was written for the issue of *Wending* devoted to Robinson.[1] Since that time much more radical books have disturbed the ecclesiastical and theological world of the Netherlands. But this does not mean that the questions which Robinson posed no longer need to be posed and answered. In any case, the confrontation with Robinson's Christology provides the occasion for illuminating the theme of this present volume from still another side.

Robinson's Valid Points

To begin with, Robinson's criticism of traditional Christology must be taken with utmost seriousness. Within the category of mythological thinking (as with Robinson, I simply take over this word from Bultmann), the conception of God the Son, who lives with God the Father from before the beginning of the world, assumes human form, preaches, suffers, dies, and rises from the dead in order again to return to the Father, can serve to indicate what is the very special significance of Jesus Christ in God's great plan for man and the world (also a mythological expression!). The "true God and true man" as it was formulated at the Council of Chalcedon gives a proper indication of the mystery of Christ—at least if one makes use of concepts like persons and natures as did the fathers who attended that council. But in the present time these concepts and ideas form just as great a hindrance for many believers and nonbelievers as the naïve idea of a God up there or a God out there.

Robinson rightly adds that the popular ecclesiastical views concerning Christ make use of the formula of Chalcedon in a one-sided way. People see Christ too much as the almighty God who walks on earth in human disguise, and they do not take his humanness seriously. A well-known Christian publishing house in the Netherlands not long ago published a paperback book of photographs of Palestine under the title *Hier heeft God gewoond* ("God lived here"). And the "Jesus Christ, God and Savior" of the World Council of Churches is one-sided also, to say the least.

We readily agree also with Robinson's praise for and criticism of the accepted liberal, free-thinking Christology. According to Robinson, it is the great merit of liberalism that it saw that the Christian faith did not need to vanish along with the supernaturalist system of thought. (Again I am using Robinson's terminology, which in this case is influenced by Tillich.) But by making Jesus the highest creature, a divinely endowed prophet, one says essentially less than does the New Testament.

When Robinson attempts to reproduce some main points of New Testament Christology, I cannot refrain from heartily underscoring what he says. In the New Testament the terms Christ and God are not interchangeable; one should take Robinson's exegesis of John 1:1 seriously.[2] Robinson rightly says that Jesus did not go about claiming to be God, but that he asked for full attention and utter obedience to what God was doing through him, indeed was doing through him in unique fashion. John 12:44-45 expresses this especially clearly. Thus Jesus reveals God, and this revelation

57

finds its climactic point in the cross. "It is in Jesus, and Jesus alone, that there is nothing of self to be seen, but solely the intimate, unconditional love of God." [3]

In this last quotation Tillich's influence is notably evident; indeed, just before this Robinson quotes him explicitly. Robinson in an interesting way then connects this central point in his argument with some intimations in Bonhoeffer's *Letters and Papers from Prison.* [4] In Jesus' surrender, in his perfect being-for-others even unto death, God is revealed. And only by having part of ourselves in this being-for-others, in this Love, can we actually believe in God.

Christ's person and work are *one*. He is fully man and fully God—not in a mysterious, indefinable connection between the natural and the supernatural, but as the incarnation (in obedience) of the transcendent God on earth, absolute Love. Herein then lies the atonement, explained as at-one-ment, the making into one of what has grown apart and become estranged. In Jesus Christ, true Being is present; in him the possibility is given us of being one with the Ground of being. In the closing pages, one quotation from Tillich follows another, and it is evident that Tillich has provided the most and the most important building blocks for Robinson's Christology.

Points of Weakness

In the last paragraph of his chapter 4, there are some splendid things which touch the heart of the matter. Yet the question must be raised as to whether Robinson, by allowing himself to be influenced too one-sidedly by the terminology of Tillich (and in part also by that of Bultmann), [5] has not neglected certain important facets of the New Testament witness. In my criticism, however, I shall be brief. Anyone who seeks to say a great deal in so short a span as does Robinson must necessarily provoke some misunderstandings. Besides, he is an exegete, not a systematic theologian. If we wish to make progress here, we shall have to pioneer in the border area between exegesis and dogmatics—and then we must correct, through gentle reproof in fraternal conversations, the one-sidedness and the mistakes of the exegetes and dogmaticians who reconnoiter in this area.

In such a conversation, then, I should like to ask the systematic theologians and my colleague Robinson whether it is precisely clear what is meant in *Honest to God* by "mythological" and "supernaturalist." I find these to be unusable characterizations of the biblical manner of thinking and speaking because they are based on later distinctions. The concept "mythological" has so many meanings that it could better be avoided.[6] The label "supernaturalism" presupposes the possibility of thinking naturalistically, and this was not present in the New Testament times, at least not present in the same way as in the eighteenth, nineteenth, or twentieth century. Further, I must confess that I do not entirely comprehend how Robinson in chapter 3 connects Tillich with Buber. If God is the Ground of all being, the Being behind and beneath all that is, if God is not a being among other beings—then it is difficult to speak about contact with him with the help of words which are borrowed from the contact between persons. Yet this is what Robinson wishes: for him the word "love" stands central. We believe in God as love, and this "means to believe that in pure personal relationship we encounter, not merely what ought to be, but what is, the deepest, veriest truth about the structure of reality."[7] That is to say that in human relationships (the being-for-others, exemplified in Jesus Christ) we see the structure of reality, the ground of being, God, illuminated. But can God actually be Love, and can love actually be love if we still prefer to speak of ground, depth, structure of reality, ultimate reality, and the unconditional? Robinson says some splendid things about God as Love, but is that not more in

59

spite of rather than thanks to the categories in which he thinks?[8] The answer to this question is of great importance for our ultimate evaluation of Robinson's Christology, which, one gets the impression, can be unfolded only within the boundaries established in his chapters on the doctrine of God.

How Shall We Advance?

But how can one honor Robinson's critique of the traditional orthodox and liberal Christological images and, inspired by his bold attempt to give a modern Christology, make further progress on one's own? The following reflections, in the main exegetical, are meant to provide some building blocks for a Christology for our time. Of course they are personally colored; that is not bad—it will never be possible to provide *the* Christology for *the* modern man. The church should not seek it in uniformity—even the New Testament, after all, knows no uniform Christology (more about this presently), and *the* modern man is a fiction.

An Experiential Christology

The only possible point of departure for a Christology lies in the biblical witnesses concerning Jesus of Nazareth. These, just as they are, without our prefixing any theory to them, must bring us to doubt, set us to thinking, urge us to introspection, until ultimately an inward assurance develops. A modern Christology will have to be experiential. We cannot pose any demands in advance for the reader of the Bible—for example, that he accept a certain doctrine of revelation, that he be convinced of the infallibility of the Scripture, or that he be ready for conversion. Subsequently it will appear that his encounter with Jesus via the biblical witnesses compels him to reflect upon revelation and the function of the Bible and that the inner readiness for conversion is necessary for a real understanding of the one who is the issue here. Of the church and of every Christian who here would prefer to intervene with theological considerations, the forbearance of Philip is asked, who, as appears from John 1:45-51, did not engage in a dispute with Nathanael over the question whether anything good could come out of Nazareth, but led his friend to Jesus. Of course this presupposes that Nathanael could surmise from Philip's words and bearing that it was worth the effort to become acquainted with Jesus.

The Necessity of Translation

The direct way to Jesus which was open to Nathanael is no longer open to us. We are finally dependent upon the testimonies of Philip and John and a great many others. These testimonies use concepts which are foreign to us and presuppose situations which are utterly different from those in which we are used to living. In one way or another, there will have to be explanation, de-mythologizing as Bultmann says (and Robinson and many others). Precisely because we may not set as a precondition for a genuine encounter with Jesus Christ the acceptance or at least the use of particular concepts out of a distant past, a particular picture of the world, or even particular religious notions of Israel or of the church, we shall be obliged to try to make the testimony transparent to what is essential. But if we do this, there is a great risk that the terminology which we use will begin to be just as much a hindrance as the old one, that it will likewise be used as a precondition and thus will hinder the experiential approach. Then Bultmann has the criticism leveled at him that he is teaching a Heideggerian Jesus, or then we say of Robinson that Tillich's patterns of thought prevent him from doing justice to the fullness of the Bible's witness. The modernists' accusations of the traditionalists are followed by the traditionalists' charges against the modernists, and of the modernists against the modernists, all of them with good reason.

61

Jesus Unique

It is good that Jesus—humanly speaking—was such a unique personality that he can be described with particular concepts, ancient or modern, but can never be comprehended in them. The unique, the unrepeatable, can never be fixed in words. This applies also to the Bible's testimony, which makes use of the conceptual material of its own time. That material, religious or nonreligious, is always simply inadequate to express what is essential. In other words, what is unique about Jesus even shines through the concepts that are used. If people had not spoken about him and if this message had not been handed on down through the ages in every possible form, then we should know nothing of Jesus. And if we do not continue to speak about him, searching, seeking, in modern concepts—as does Bultmann or Bonhoeffer or Robinson—then we fall short. Jesus can tolerate the testimony that is given concerning him. Not only because of but also in spite of the testimony he comes to us. Even where the God of the church has long since been declared to be dead, he continues to grip people, and he is reverenced. Even nonbelievers bear witness concerning him, as indeed we have known since the man of Gadara (Mark 5:17), Caiaphas' judgment, and Pilate's shrugging of his shoulders.

Recoining the Language

A modern Christology then will also be able to begin with an analysis of the many points on which in the New Testament the images are inadequate or must be reshaped, where speaking has become stuttering, where different expressions correct each other, and a multiplicity of titles still appear not to be able ultimately to express what is unique about Jesus. Not only is this analysis extremely fascinating, but it also tends to make us more modest with respect to our own conceptual material. The uniqueness of this man in his relation to God and to people, and of the new life which he proposes to give us, breaks through all the concepts and images that are employed, accepting them and rejecting them at the same time. Our language is serviceable for the proclamation only if it is recoined.[9]

Implicit Christology

In view of the experiential character of Christology, it is good first of all to analyze those passages in which something is said about a direct encounter of Jesus with a person or a group of persons. There Jesus' authority always appears in practice because he reveals a man to himself and confronts him with a decision. In the story of the rich young man (Mark 10:17-27 and parallels), the Christological significance is not to be found solely or even primarily in the beginning verses 17 and 18 ("Why do you call me good? There is none good but God alone").[10] The important thing is the absolute authority with which in the strictly personal encounter with this young man one particular commandment is inculcated. This man saw himself and discovered what authentic humanness for him needed to include; he heard God in Jesus' words just as he had heard him in Moses' law. His decision was negative, and Jesus' disciples realized why. They knew themselves to be placed, with the young man, before an impossible decision because their empirical humanness too was being measured against the authentic humanness with which they were confronted in their Master. As is seen from what follows, authentic humanness can only be given (not earned) and gratefully received. The genuine humanness is set forth in Jesus' word and bearing; to believe means to let oneself be brought into the movement toward the man who here becomes visible and audible.

Here I have deliberately used terms which Robinson also employs because I think they are eminently usable. The gospel brings man to reflection on what it means to be human, on his

63

very personal existence. In this anthropology a Christology is concealed because of the authority of the word which decisively influences our reflection and because of the exemplary life in which this word functions, the significance also of Jesus' deeds themselves and of his final deed, his giving of himself on the cross.

In many respects this implicit Christology is more important than the explicit, which makes use of theological arguments and existing concepts (experientially reshaped, of course). Yet our decision, our experience, our *de facto* assent, will compel a thinking through and a formulating of our own relationship to Jesus and of Jesus' relationship to God.

God as Person

With this last point we come to a very difficult problem, if we take seriously Robinson's critique of the God up there and out there and at the same time doubt whether his view of God as the deep Ground of our being helps us along the way. It appears to me that the important point is whether the terms which we have used have a referential character. They must not lock God up within a human philosophy. Here personal and impersonal categories are equally dangerous. One can speak of God so personally that he becomes *a* God, a particular individual among other individuals; then one falls into a veneration of an image that he himself has created and thus into idolatry. And then the critique of the God up there or out there can have the effect of a cleansing, purifying, shattering of images. One can also speak of God so impersonally that a genuinely personal relationship to this God appears to belong to the realm of impossibility. He is so lofty, so deep or so remote that he is turned into a vaguely delineated It. Vital piety which is guided by the Bible demands a very personal relationship to God.

How does the Bible, which even in its theological utterances

64

places so very much emphasis upon the personal relationship to God, guard against image worship? It does this by using a great many personal relationships as suggestions and by constantly letting it be noted that God is simply different. In Isaiah 40:12-31, for example, one figure is heaped on another, without God's being "locked in" to them. The prophet here clearly is concerned with the incomparability of God, precisely in his very intensively personal concern with Israel. God is the Father *and* the judge *and* the farmer *and* the king, and so on. And again he is always all this precisely in a way different from a man in the same role. We read it and are amazed by it. He shatters our images and transcends them, while we yet may maintain a very personal relationship to him. Indeed, precisely because he is so different, the personal relationship is for us fundamental and unique: the one pearl for which we may sell all our possessions (Matt. 13:45-46).

It is interesting and instructive that in the Bible impersonal figures are also used, for God and even for Jesus. In the New Testament this occurs, for example, in the Johannine literature. In the prologue to the Fourth Gospel, "word" is found along with "life" and "light"; and Jesus' earthly nature is typified by "glory," "grace," and "truth." In John 15, the Father is the farmer, and Jesus is the vine. The disciples remain united with him as branches with the vine, but at the same time they are also his friends. In John 17 the boundaries of what is conceivable are overstepped and every comparison is relativized: for example, in verse 21: "as thou, Father, art in me and I in thee, that they also may be in us" and verse 23: "I in them and thou in me, that they may be made perfect in one, so that the world may recognize that thou hast sent me and that thou has loved them as thou hast loved me." All this is very personal, and yet at the same time it transcends what is human and limited in our ideas concerning personal relationships. Yet John does not fall into a mysticism of being wherein impersonal expressions are preferred in order to

65

give expression to the hiddenness of the human in the divine being (although his words are often misunderstood in this sense).

Still more biblical examples could be given, but what has just been noted, together with what was said in sections 3 and 4 above, will have made it clear that in speaking about God in personal terms we do need to be cautious, but not convulsively so. Above all, it should say that any Christology ought to be inspired by the Bible to great flexibility and originality in the use of language and that it will be obliged to treasure diversity in approach and manner of expression as a high and indispensable good.

Up There

Particular attention must be given to the connection between the picture of the world and the view of God. Does not the Bible then think of God as "up there," in a spatial sense, because it conceives of the universe as three-storied? The biblical writers use the picture of the world that belongs to their time, and it is inescapably evident that for them heaven is a place above, far away. Jesus' ascension is presented in Acts 1:9-11 in realistic terms: Jesus is taken up and carried away on a cloud. His return to earth will take place in the same way.

In the visions of the book of Revelation spatial conceptions are not shunned. (How would it even have been possible to avoid them?) Yet here also the referential character of these conceptions, which are more or less bound up with the world-view, is evident. Even assuming that it would be possible to fix the various visions in the last book of the Bible, each one separately, in film (which would demand that the photographer see much more than the author of the Apocalypse, who expressed his vision in words), still the multiplicity and the rapid changing of the pictures would not give any person viewing the film the idea that now he knows how heaven or the throne or the Lamb (Christ) looks—let alone that he should think that God was fixed in that place, spatially speaking.

Further, only the beginning of Acts describes Jesus' ascension with spatial ideas and concepts. Matt. 28 says nothing about an ascension, but the last word has to do with the nearness of the Lord: "I am with you always, to the end of the world" (vs. 20). In John the matter is difficult and subtle, but if we compare 20:17-18 with 20:19-29, we must come to the conclusion that the "ascending to the Father" (vs. 17) is seen as the final note of Jesus' victory over hate and death and at the same time it is seen as the beginning of a new, deepened, strengthened fellowship of the community with her Lord. And one last indication: when Paul, in the earliest account of the resurrection that we have (I Cor. 15:1-11), places the appearances of Jesus to his disciples on the same plane with Jesus' meeting Paul himself on the Damascus road, one may not say that Paul is giving a strained conception of matters because he places himself on the same plane with the other apostles; but then one must draw from this the conclusion that the spatial conceptions which he and his readers connected with resurrection and return to the Father did not form any hindrances to this equating of the appearances. Jesus' departure to go to the Father does not stand in the way of his being near his disciples, an inward connection of Lord and church. On this point also the images and terms used are in principle shattered and relativized through their being related to these entirely unique realities and relations. Thus this in turn has to say to us that in the use of spatial conceptions we may be cautious and confident at the same time!

Jesus' Referential Humanness

We return now to the point that was noted above. The relationship of man to the man Jesus is a very personal one, and by means of the referential character of Jesus' life man may stand in a very personal relationship to God—a relationship about which we may think and speak in personal terms as previously described. Every breakthrough and correction of the view of Jesus and of God, in dealing with the Bible, with the tradition of the church (and the world), and with present-day believers (and nonbelievers) will unavoidably have as a result the revision also of the view of man. We are constantly compelled to review our attitude of life and our theology. Believers are people who are on the way, ever since Abraham, indeed, ever since Adam and Eve were driven out of the shelter of the garden of Eden.

Jesus' relationship to God (and to men) here is revelatory and exemplary. We must take Jesus' humanness seriously. He too was a man on the way, he had to discover the divine "must." It was not revealed to him before the beginning of time as his inescapable lot. Instead, he had to gain the insight into it and the surrender to it in inward struggle (Gethsemane). Precisely in his genuine, complete humanness God is revealed. On this point we can learn from Bonhoeffer. We must not try to emphasize the divine in Jesus, let alone localize it; of itself it comes to the fore in what is human. Even the human finite—how could Jesus ever be believable as a child of God if he had not also been a child of his time?

Atonement

The encounter with God in Jesus Christ reveals the distance between man's actual life and his commission and destiny. The cross in many different ways impresses upon us how great is the distance and how deep the cleft. At the same time it proclaims to us how near God means to stay to the men who are alienated and estranged from him. In our thinking about the resurrection we shall have to place heavy emphasis on the fact that the reports about it are not written out of a biological, physical, or metaphysical interest, but that they are intended precisely to show the concrete closeness, the irresistible power, and the marvelous constancy of God's loving concern with and for men. The fountain of authentic humanity, opened up in Jesus' human existence, continues to flow: "The water which I shall give him shall become in him a fountain of water that springs up to eternal life" (John 4:14). One should not speak of the resurrection theoretically, but practically, with the eye upon the new life and from the perspective of that new life that is manifested in the company of those who are united to Jesus Christ.

In this connection Robinson, following Tillich, writes about estrangement and reconciliation. The New Testament here uses many concepts and figures which also accentuate other elements in the God-man relationship. These often can be understood only against the background of the Old Testament and then-current usages—in which connection it once again is true that what is similar as well as what is entirely different, the element of fulfillment as well as that of detachment and revision, must be emphasized. For example, it speaks of forgiveness, healing, liberation, atonement (in the sense of the restoration of a relationship as well as with a cultic significance), justification, sanctification, admission to a new alliance. Here too the figures of speech stumble over each other, correct each other, and an abundance of Old Testament texts are used for elucidation. It is always the same reality that is involved, but this selfsame reality does again and again exhibit new facets. There is not any such thing as a doctrine of the atonement which with some exposition and some modernizing could be rendered ready-made for present-day use. Any authentically modern Christology will have to go *ad fontes*—back to the Bible and back to the sources of genuine humanness in relationship to the living God. In our doing so it could appear that the old concepts which are bound to a bygone historical situation cannot simply be repeated; that would do wrong to their referential character. But then it will also become evident that neither may they be pushed aside as obsolete—this also because of their

69

referential character. Only when we take seriously the historical nature both of these concepts and of contemporary man will this part of Christology be able really to be modern. Moreover, this of course is only a suggestion of the possibilities; the important thing is to work out these possibilities.

God's Future

In conclusion, there is one more motif in Christology which I should like to bring out, namely the eschatological. Robinson does not deal with this; he shares[11] the opinion of many English New Testament scholars that in Jesus' life and instruction all the emphasis lay on the present fulfillment and process of being fulfilled of the expectation of the Jewish people (realized eschatology). Only later, in early Christianity, is a renewed expectation of the future said to have found a place, and this is said then also to have colored the New Testament descriptions of Jesus' works and acts. Along with many others, I regard this view as untenable for both historical and exegetical reasons. Besides, it fails to appreciate the tension between essential and actual humanness, which is emphasized precisely in Jesus' bearing and his dealing with man, the nation, and the world. The important point is the realization of the new, authentic humanity not only in the individual life but also in the common humanity in all sorts of relationships of life. Man is man on the way, a pilgrim, and the world is a world on the way, a pilgrim world. God has set us on our way and has made it clear to us that there is no turning back. Just as we, with Bonhoeffer and Robinson, wish to place all emphasis on worldly holiness, the holiness which the world itself puts into practice will have to concern us. God is not God only of and for the Christians. He is the Lord and the Ground of all being. Hence it is that the New Testament looks forward to the city at the end of the way of humanity, of which Rev. 21:22-26 says figuratively: ''And I saw no temple in the city, for its temple is the Lord

God Almighty and the Lamb. And the city has no need of sun or moon to shine upon it, for the glory of God is its light, and its lamp is the Lamb. By its light shall the nations walk; and the kings of the earth shall bring their glory into it, and its gates shall never be shut by day—and there shall be no night there; they shall bring into it the glory and the honor of the nations'' (RSV).

V

Jesus as Man Among Men

Introduction

"There are situations where it is superhuman to keep going, simply to keep going. He, he was not superhuman; I can assure you that. He screamed out his fear of death, but that is just why I love him, this is why he became my friend, he who died without ultimately knowing."[1]

Thus speaks Clamence, the main character in Albert Camus' work, *The Fall,* about Jesus.[2] He alludes to Jesus' cry on the cross which is related by Mark (15:34) and Matthew (27:46): "My God, my God, why hast thou forsaken me?" Jesus perished for the needs of the world, in which world he lived thanks to the death of many: "The Jewish children who were killed in the slaughter of the innocents at Bethlehem, while his parents took him to a safe place, why did they die? Was it not for his sake?" He could no longer go on living if it "is an infinitely greater crime to remain alive than to allow the lives of others to be taken." Day after day he had before his eyes a crime of which he himself was innocent, and therefore he went away, in order somewhere else to find help and understanding. He did not find this help there. Mark and Matthew are honest enough to report this, too, but Luke has excised this cry.

Camus loves Jesus and regards him as his friend precisely as a man who also could not go on, who fell beneath this burden. He has no use for a superhuman being. The church's Son of God, addressed with many fine titles and adorned with all sorts of predicates of divinity, imperturbable in his union with God, remains remote and foreign to Camus. The victim on the cross is his friend, precisely in his defeat.

. It would be worth the effort more closely to analyze Camus' views concerning guilt, justification, judgment, and forgiveness. For the moment I shall only remark that Camus' words, apart from the broader context in which they are used, interpret what many feel. Theological concepts and biblical terms have become opaque. What once served to express what was fully distinctive about Jesus now serves as a hindrance to many. The man Jesus is pictured as a *super*human being, and now appears as not human.[3] His cross, however, remains a cross; he died as one condemned to death, trapped by his enemies, abandoned by his friends. As the crucified man of Nazareth he stands closer to us than as the risen Lord. As the crucified one he is genuinely human, as the resurrected one incomprehensible and vague.

It Began with a Human Encounter

Let us not forget that for the first disciples and enemies of Jesus an ordinary human encounter with him was the beginning of their trust and of their rejection of him, an encounter which involved an appeal, a call to a decision. The stories which are told about this in the gospels make it clear to us that there could be no talk of neutrality. And there can be no such talk, because when we listen well, we discover that we ourselves are Peter or Nathanael, John the Baptist or Pilate, and that we ourselves play a role in Jesus' parables.

In the history of which Jesus of Nazareth is the central figure, the little life story of many others is involved. And, to use a saying of Amos N. Wilder, those who are involved are not only Peter, John, and Thomas, but also Tom, Dick, and Harry.[4] We do not find ourselves in all the stories, nor always in the same story; but we always are somewhere confronted with the question of who we are and what we therefore ought to do. In each of the gospel narratives Jesus stands at the center, as a genuine man, not as a God in human disguise. It is true that in his words men hear a summons or a promise from God—but that is something else. Indeed there also are those who see demonic forces at work in him. However, no one who actually hears and really uses his eyes can remain neutral.

Jesus was indeed a special man; when he spoke, his words did something, and when he acted, something happened. The ones who were addressed in that speaking and acting were affected and were constrained to respond and to act. In the encounter a crisis took place, *the* crisis (of decision, judgment) without parallel, says the Gospel of John. In the decision of the person with respect to this Jesus the judgment upon his own life is passed.

When he speaks, fishermen leave their nets (Mark 1:16-20), and a tax collector leaves his office (2:13-17), and family ties become unimportant (3:31-35). He is turned away from his village as a young man who thinks too highly of himself (6:1-6) or is hailed as the awaited "Anointed of the Lord" (8:27-30). A young man who (according to his own account) has done all that God asks is confronted with the question whether he really is willing to give up everything for God (10:17-22), and the disciples who own not a single penny comprehend that this is just as difficult for them as for the rich young man (10:23-27). This Jesus talks with Pharisees, with followers of Herod, and with Sadducees (12:13-27), and there is no one who can corner him, not because he is so clever but because he knows how to penetrate to the heart of the matter. "And no one dared to ask him anything more"

(12:34). As at the very first, in Capernaum, they were always astonished at his teaching, "for he taught them as one having authority and not as the scribes" (Mark 1:22).

And the Miracles, Then?

One could counter with the question: why, in the summary just given, were the healings and the other miracles not mentioned? When Jesus spoke, people were healed, physically and mentally. Do not these signs indicate that Jesus is more than an ordinary man, a son of God, the Son of God?

For the others who participated in the drama in which Jesus was the main character, the unusual deeds of Jesus were indeed of the greatest importance, precisely because *there* also it was evident how his words and deeds form a unity. "You dumb and deaf spirit, I command you, come out of him, and never enter him again. And . . . it came out" (Mark 9:25-26 RSV). But Jesus' disciples saw the deeds and did not use them as proofs of Jesus' deity.

I leave aside the question of precisely what happened, and of how much the various stories have grown or have been tampered with in the retelling. It is obvious that for those whom Jesus had encountered these stories formed an essential part of the great story of his life, but that therein the miracles function as indicators and not as proofs.

Take, for example, the story in Mark 3:22-27 and parallels. Jesus' opponents do not deny his healings; he does indeed drive out evil spirits. The question is only: how can he do this? The opponents say that he does it "by the prince of demons." Jesus' disciples believe that it is the powers given by God that are at work in Jesus, and they interpret his healings as signs of the great in-breaking of the kingdom of light into the domain of darkness. God's kingdom, long expected and often foretold, now stands at the door: it is already present in the singular unity of the word and deed of this man Jesus. "The time is fulfilled, and the kingdom of God is at hand. Repent and believe the gospel" (1:15).

Their interpretation is an interpretation in faith—they give this explanation on the basis of their affirmative response to Jesus; from this fundamental yes they see these deeds otherwise than do the opponents from their fundamental no, and they also read the Scriptures, which they have in common with the opponents, differently; all sorts of prophecies can now be meaningfully related to what happens here (see, for example, the discussion between Jesus and John the Baptist, reported in Matt. 11:2-6). But there is no thought of proof. In and of itself the explanation given by the opponents is also plausible. In any case Jesus was not an ordinary man—but he does not need therefore to be divine; quite the contrary.

The Gospel of John, which constantly poses matters still more sharply than do the first three gospels and follows out every problem to its essential issue, clearly makes a distinction between two kinds of seeing. In a conversation with the Jews, which he has after he has fed the five thousand, Jesus says: "I know very well why you are seeking me; it is not because you have seen signs, but because you were able to eat as much bread as you wanted" (John 6:26). One can also hear in different ways. When Jesus announces his death, and sees his dying as the way which he must go in order to give God the honor that rightly belongs to him, a voice sounds from heaven which identifies Jesus as preeminently God's servant, who himself may share in the divine glory (12:27-28). But some of the bystanders said that it thundered, and others declared that an angel had spoken to him. They did not hear what was there to be heard, just as the Jews in chapter 6 had not seen what was there to be seen. As a believer, John knows that in Jesus God himself has spoken to men. "The Word became flesh and dwelt among us," he says in John 1:14, and he adds that we (the believers) have seen the divine majesty with which he, as the only Son of the Father, was clothed, full of grace and truth. All that God had to say, he communicated in this special member of the human family. No one else uses such exalted terms to speak of Jesus as does John—but yet he knows very well that this Jesus was fully and entirely man.

In John 6 there is represented a major and definitive division among Jesus' disciples. Some say, "That is much too difficult; who can listen to it?" (vs. 60), and go away. Speaking for those who remain faithful, Simon Peter says, "What you are saying is eternal life. We believe, we know that you are God's holy one" (vss. 68-69). Simon and the others are talking about the very same words of Jesus, and they have witnessed the very same deeds.

Cross and Resurrection

Thus even for the eyewitnesses—or, better, the participants in the history of which Jesus is the center—faith remains faith. What they see and hear awakens faith (in the sense of insight and trust), strengthens faith, corrects faith, but for genuine seeing and true hearing, at least a beginning of faith is necessary. It remains an interaction, because seeing, hearing, and believing function only in the encounter of man and man, of the man Jesus and the others, who at last say yes to him with their whole lives. Also only within the framework of this encounter and on the basis of obedience to the summons which is sounded within it is the quoting of expressions from the Scripture convincing, and only here may one point to Jesus as the one in whom God's kingdom is beginning to be realized on earth.

From the Gospels and the Epistles of the New Testament it is evident that the sufferings of Jesus and his death on the cross confronted those who had accepted him as Lord with great difficulties. When Paul writes that the crucified Christ is for the Jews

77

a stumbling block (a reason for unbelief) and for the Gentiles foolishness, but that those who are called, both Jews and Greeks, discover and encounter in him power and wisdom (I Cor. 1:23-24), he is speaking retrospectively. He is saying this out of the conviction of faith that this Jesus is indeed the one sent by God, and that therefore his sufferings and death are willed by God and fit into God's plan for the world. And then, as is evident from other passages from his epistles, he also learned to interpret this death with the help of a number of passages from the Scripture the meaning of which he had not been able previously to understand thus.

The Gospels, likewise written later on, do not conceal the fact that the disciples were unable to do anything with the sufferings and the cross when Jesus spoke to them earlier about these matters and that they were bewildered when their master was actually taken prisoner and put to death. It is equally obvious that in fact they shrank back from giving the testimony which the crucified Jesus asked of them as their response. "Whoever among you wishes to be first is to be the servant of all. For the Son of Man has not come to be served but to serve and to give his life a ransom for many" (Mark 10:44-45).

Jesus was so genuinely human that he really died. Therefore he is my friend, says Camus. Jesus felt himself abandoned by God. At the last this was all he knew, Camus says, and this is why I love him.

For the disciples, who also loved him and who called him more than friend, who had heard God speaking and had seen him acting in Jesus, the cross was a riddle, because they could not harmonize this death with God's acting. Later they understood that even in his human demise the man Jesus was compelling them to begin thinking differently about God, that in Jesus' words and deeds before his crucifixion there were all sorts of reference points for a faith perspective on the cross, and that precisely where everything is snatched from a person's hands and faith is put to the test, that faith can be deepened.

Even here the trust of faith and the insight of faith remain bound to the relationship of the believing (and doubting) person to the man Jesus. But then the resurrection? Does not the New Testament tell us of Jesus' victory over death—of the empty tomb, and of new encounters with his disciples? Do we not then have to do here with a clearly discernible and verifiable intervention on God's part, a proof of Jesus' deity? What was said about the stories of the miracles applies also to the stories concerning the resurrection. It is difficult to trace out what actually happened. Cullmann rightly emphasizes the fact that the resurrection event in itself cannot be historically verified and moreover that it is nowhere described in the gospel narratives. It is true that the accompanying phenomena are described, but of these it must be said that the proclamation of the resurrection gives only one possible explanation.[5] The empty tomb can also be explained by the theft of Jesus' body by the disciples (Matt. 28:11-15), and the appearances of Jesus were restricted to encounters with his followers (Acts 10:40 ff. says: he did not appear to all the people but to us who were chosen to bear witness to him). Various biblical passages make it evident that it was difficult for the disciples to believe the message of the resurrection. In the story of the travelers to Emmaus (Luke 24:13-35), it appears that for these disciples of Jesus the opening of the Scriptures (the making transparent of all sorts of statements from the Old Testament in their significance for the present) must be coupled with the opening of the eyes (vss. 31, 32). Before that, they do not recognize Jesus in the stranger who is walking beside them.

Even where the resurrection is concerned, event and faith are related to each other. It is no easier to say "yes" to the risen Lord than to the crucified Jesus; a relationship of trust to the resurrected One presupposes that one accepts him as the crucified One.

The Early Christian Proclamation

Those who felt themselves compelled to tell about Jesus, to preach, did this as people who had participated with all their being in the events around Jesus. They spoke out of an encounter which had been decisive for their own acting and speaking, and tried by means of their words to bring others to the same encounter. The written word (in the Gospels, for example) goes back to the direct, living, spoken word and seeks to bring people to a face-to-face encounter—thus A. N. Wilder[6]—a person-to-person encounter with Jesus. Most of the people who met Jesus had definite ideas about God; they had been brought up in more or less religious families within the Jewish tradition; they interpreted what they heard and saw in terms of particular ideas, borrowed from the Old Testament and developed under the influence of all sorts of events in the history of the Jewish people and of ideas from without as well. In this respect also Jesus himself was a child of his times and of his people.

But the words of Jesus again and again break through what is given in tradition, and the events again and again take a surprising turn; they compel people to think and act differently—in short, to be converted. And thus people, rooted in the tradition, come to unexpected interpretations and to an entirely new use of the data of Scripture and tradition.

Words were recoined and acquired a special connotation from the encounter with Jesus, who spoke as no one had ever spoken before and whose life and words formed a unity. A. N. Wilder speaks of a "language-shaping faith," supported by "a particular life-experience," and he appropriates Ernst Fuchs' term *Sprachereignis*. In Jesus' preaching and in the preaching about him something happens, the language is reshaped and is put to work to add a new dimension to people's views of themselves and of the world.[7] Answering to this new hearing and this new understanding is a new life, both personal and in association with those who know themselves to be addressed.

Jesus is the Messiah; yes, to be sure, but *he* is the Messiah. He may be called the Son of Man—but he is this in *his own* way. When Jesus begins to explain (according to Mark 8:31-33 and parallels) that suffering awaits him, Peter, who has just called him Messiah, finds it necessary to take him aside and show him how foolish this expectation is. Peter does not understand that Jesus is the Messiah in his own way and that he himself, in the concrete encounter with Jesus, thus must revise his ideas concerning the one who is sent by God and concerning God himself. And not only his dogmatics, but his whole attitude of life must change. "If anyone will come after me, let him deny himself and take up his cross and follow me" (Mark 8:34).

Thus people come to the proclamation of the good news. "But it is Good News of a total and ultimate kind, and not only recited but effectively and dynamically demonstrated." [8]

The early Christian proclamation is an indispensable link in our encounter with Jesus.[9] Those who told the stories and the gospel-writers who collected them, edited them, and put them together in the form of gospels, tried to let Jesus himself speak, but of course in their handing down of his words and deeds their own reaction to these also spoke. We ought to see clearly and to respect fully the human aspects of the process of tradition which led to our four gospels. We may even rejoice in the fact that the man Jesus even now can still address us through human ears, hearts, and mouths.

Therefore we may critically but affirmatively accept the results of modern biblical scholarship which approaches the Bible as a collection of writings in which people give expression in the most diverse ways to what has affected them. We may take into account the timebound elements, the human limitations, and the historical accidents which have played a role in the tradition. We need to have our eyes open to the diversity in the tradition: each one spoke in his own way about what filled his heart, and the evangelists brought together various sorts of tradition material: stories told to outsiders, catechism pieces, hymns and confessions of faith, detached sayings, and so on. Therewith they composed their own gospels, however much they attempted to give the good news about Jesus. In this variety is reflected the wealth and richness of the new life and new discourse that arose out of the encounter with Jesus.

We must also take into account the fact that in the tradition much is added, omitted, or adapted to the situation in which a particular story functioned. Everything that lives grows, adapts itself; only what is dead remains the same. Of course we know Jesus only as his contemporaries saw him. It is fortunate that so many people saw and heard him and spoke about him in so many ways. Of course we must critically analyze the elements in the tradition, try to show their place in the process of tradition in order then to evaluate them in their peculiarity. But what is late and perhaps not at all spoken or done by Jesus as reported is not necessarily untrue. I cite Wilder again: ''Jesus' creative speech was so fresh and significant that it could, as it were, breed speech true to itself.'' [10] He then uses the example of Abraham Lincoln, about whom so many stories are circulated, which probably are not authentic but nevertheless are true to Lincoln.

Our Speaking About Jesus

Now when we try to draw some lines from the foregoing argument to our preaching, we can note the following:

a) It is just as necessary to speak about Jesus in words of our own time and to seek forms of Christian life and society that are suited to our time as it is wrong to want to be modern at whatever cost. Our new speaking will be able to be both new and renewing

82

only when it goes back to the source and thus arises out of our own encounter with Jesus—an encounter not in a mystical or pietistic or light romantic fashion, but on the basis of a studying and a living through of what is new in Jesus' speaking and in the preaching of his followers. It holds true for us also that a language-shaping faith presupposes a particular life experience. Even modern language will have to be reforged and modern philosophical methods of approach as well, regardless of whether they are borrowed from German or French existentialism or from the various currents of analytical philosophy. Our words are only partly usable to trace out the truth about Jesus.

Genuine life breaks through the language. It is not a bad thing when you begin stammering, and it is better ultimately to be eloquently silent than to drown out one's own voice (and Jesus).

b) We shall have to return constantly to the Bible and because the issue is the encounter with Jesus, especially to the New Testament.

We must approach this in the way indicated in the preceding section and steer clear of all ideas of a doctrine about God or a doctrine about Jesus' relationship to the Father and of the relationship of the divine to the human in Jesus, which are supposed to be derived from the New Testament and in the course of church history have been derived from it. It is possible that sometime we shall try to arrive at a systematic thinking through and ordering of the various aspects of Jesus' speaking and acting. Man has been charged to serve God with his understanding also; it is here that theology finds its justification. However, speculation about the being, the nature of Jesus, using the concepts of classical metaphysics threatens so heavily to accentuate the superhuman and supernatural that the humanly creative character of Jesus is obscured.

c) However, it is not only the classical dogmatic terms, but also the biblical way of speaking that stands in our way. The believers

83

of the New Testament describe Jesus with the help of theological words and concepts of their time and of their country. How could they have done otherwise? The man Jesus plays his role in God's dealing with men that began with the creation and ends with the consummation. But the anthropomorphic terminology, the talk about a God who acts, rewards, punishes, forgives, and intervenes in our lives, no longer serves. The existence of God has become a problem—not because people have consciously become unbelievers, but because the word "God" as such no longer functions. This word no longer conveys any meaning, or, better said, with it people can only connect conceptions which appear obsolete, childish, or irrelevant.

In his *The Secular Meaning of the Gospel,* [11] Paul van Buren has attempted to talk about God in a radically worldly fashion. He says that faith witnesses are not utterances about metaphysical facts or events, but utterances which give expression to a particular view of the world, of one's fellowman, and of one's own self, a view which is also concretized in a particular manner of life. In other words, we must see these utterances as expressions of believing people. And if we inquire still further for the source from which this view arises, we read in the New Testament that Jesus' life, death, and resurrection have given the Christians this perspective. "Whatever men were looking for in looking for 'God,' is to be found by finding Jesus of Nazareth." [12]

A discussion with van Buren must begin with a discussion of his philosophical points of departure. Whatever may be the results to which this discussion leads, it is evident, I think, that his method of approach offers a fruitful point of departure. To begin with, then, let us leave off all expressions about God and concern ourselves intensively with the reports about Jesus and with the way in which believers spoke about him and lived out of the encounter with him. Van Buren himself says that his method of approach means a reduction, but it is a healthy reduction, one

84

demanded by the times. He regards it as a reduction to what is essential and says: "The path we have described for the secular Christian in the secular world is clear and wide enough to carry the whole Gospel along it." [13]

This last remains to be seen—but if the path needs to be widened, this will become evident as we go our way as prescribed. To be concerned with Jesus and to share with his followers in their encounter with him and their reflection about him involve also being concerned with their manner of speaking and thinking. And it is possible that then in this old manner of speaking the truth may yet suddenly so dawn that we prefer this old manner of speaking to a new, empirically verifiable, secular style of expression. To put it in another way, poets and prophets can say more with words than philosophers and theologians can discover in them by means of cool analysis.

VI

Theology as Narration

Introduction

This chapter too is concerned with a number of aspects of the early Christian discourse about Jesus and about God.[1] It is limited to that part of the early Christian tradition (in the sense of handing on the faith witness) that has found its written deposit in the New Testament, and it places special emphasis on the fact that in this tradition the narrative plays a major role. In this connection grateful use is made of the stimulating book *The Language of the Gospel: Early Christian Rhetoric,* by A. N. Wilder,[2] which has already been cited several times in the preceding chapter.

Added to the historical exposition are some comments which are intended to stimulate the reader to think through the question to what extent this aspect of the early Christian tradition can point the direction for contemporary speaking about Jesus and about God.

Jesus and Israel

The early Christian authors whose writings are handed down in the New Testament describe Jesus' life, death, and resurrection as an essential and decisive episode in God's concern with Israel, with the nations, and indeed with the whole creation. People could not speak of Jesus without speaking of God, that is, about Yahweh, and conversely, after the encounter with Jesus they could no longer speak of God without taking into account what was said and done in and through Jesus.

We find a clear example of this in I John, an epistle directed against those who deny the humanity of Jesus Christ and think that they are able to know God without acknowledging the concrete human existence of Jesus. The author sets himself against this misunderstanding at once in his introduction, I John 1:1-4, which is intended to dot the *i*'s for the (still) faithful members of the community by impressing on them the fact that only in fellowship with Jesus, realized in the fellowship with each other, does fellowship with God come into being.

Hence the "we have heard . . . seen . . . handled . . . we proclaim to you"—thus there is koinonia[3] between you and ourselves, and through us also koinonia with the Father and his Son Jesus Christ. True joy lies therein, and therefrom issues the true life.

Now what is seen, heard, and handed down? The Life (I John 1:2), the Word, the Light (John 1:1-18), but in Jesus. "For the law was given through Moses; grace and truth came through Jesus" (John 1:17). Hence even in a quite late stage of the tradition, after the other Gospels had already come into being, in the circle of John also a Gospel was written in which God's speaking and acting in Jesus of Nazareth stand central. There is in this Gospel a tendency to stress the distance between what is totally new in the deeds, the words, and the entire being of Jesus of Nazareth and the current Jewish conceptions and expectations. The group of communities for whom "John" writes is evidently in continuing conversation (perhaps we could better say "debate") with Jewish groups who reject Jesus. Yet it becomes evident throughout the Fourth Gospel that this new element, and much else besides, can be explained only with the help of points of departure and lines of argument which were shared with the Jews.

It is essential to recognize that Jesus is sent by God, that he is related to God in a unique way, and that he thus does not speak on his own authority (of himself).[4] One could think that John is interested solely in the vertical line of connection between Father and Son. But John 1:1-18, in which the ''from above downward'' gets all the attention, is immediately followed by John 1:19-51, where there is explicit discussion of the place of Jesus in the history of Israel (and of his relationship with John the Baptist, who had already been mentioned in the prologue). It is noticeable how in the conversations mentioned in John 1, again and again concepts that are important for the Jewish expectations come to the fore (''the Messiah'' in verse 41; ''he of whom Moses in the law and the prophets have written'' in verse 45; ''the Son of God, the king of Israel'' in verse 49; ''the Son of Man'' in verse 51). R. Schnackenburg correctly says that this passage is concerned with ''presenting Jesus as the promised Messiah whom Israel hoped for from among its sons, and at the same time, as the eschatological saviour who surpasses all expectations and can be confessed only in new categories.'' [5]

History and Faith

Only on the basis of a faith decision does one see the proper connection between the history of Jesus and God's history with Israel, the nations, and the world. The seeing and hearing in I John 1:1-4 change faith and lead to faith (moreover, faith is thereby strengthened and/or corrected). The disciples of Jesus who go away saying that ''that is much too difficult, no one can heed that'' (John 6:60) have at their disposal precisely the same facts as does Simon Peter, who in the name of those who remain faithful says, "What you are saying is eternal life. We believe, we know that you are God's holy one" (John 6:68). It is only in faith that they are in a position to interpret these facts differently (and, in the conviction of the early Christians, correctly). Jesus' words and deeds remain within the circle of revelation and faith (John 12:37, 44-50). One cannot naïvely explain that it ought to be evident to everyone that "in former times God spoke frequently and in diverse ways to the fathers through the prophets" and that "in these last days he has spoken to us in the Son" (Heb. 1:1). Nor was the early church so naïve—she saw clearly that the affirmation as well as the denial of the view of the writer of Hebrews involves a decision. Nevertheless, she had to reckon with the hard fact that Jerusalem had not discerned what belonged to her peace, because it remained hidden from her eyes (Luke 19:42). Again, it is John who states the matter plainly when he has Jesus say, "You have seen me and yet you do not believe. But all that the Father gives to me shall come to me; and whoever comes to me I will not reject. For I have come from heaven, not to do what I will, but to do the will of him who sent me" (John 6:36-38). Here then again fits the emphasis on the faith witness of those in I John 1:1-4 who have been enabled to see and hear: the church lives by that witness, that committed speaking of an event in which people themselves are involved and by which people are themselves compelled to make a decision (thus also John 20:30-31).

What holds true of the Gospel of John and the First Epistle of John also holds true of all that the Christianity of the first century has handed down to us by way of epistles, narratives, hymns, bits of preaching material, words of Jesus, and so forth; it is all marked by the faith of the early church in all her variations. We shall have to give due regard to what tradition-critical *(traditionsgeschichtliche)* studies have to tell us about how the testimony concerning the story of Jesus was handed down. These studies have reference to the smallest units, handed down primarily in the oral tradition (''Form-Criticism,'' *Formgeschichte)* as well as to the composition and the theological aim of larger units (''Redaction-Criticism,'' *Redaktionsgeschichte).*[6]

How Did People Speak of Jesus?

With reference to the tradition in the Synoptic Gospels (to which we limit ourselves in this section), it has already long ago been noted by form critics such as M. Dibelius and R. Bultmann that these made use of stereotyped forms, mostly brief stories and various types of sayings of Jesus. A twofold division is possible, into narrative material *(Haggadah)* and discourse material *(Halakhah).* The first longer narrative that arose, constructed out of smaller units, was the passion narrative, in which the faith perspective on the cross is given and it is made clear why all this had to happen.[7] One should note how closely narrative and saying therein are frequently connected. In the short narratives, which Dibelius calls paradigms and Bultmann calls apophthegms, a saying of Jesus stands central, and the narrative is focused entirely upon this saying. One may read, for example, Mark 12:13-17, where a number of Pharisees and Herodians ask Jesus whether it is lawful to pay taxes to Caesar, and this leads to the ''Render unto Caesar what is Caesar's and unto God what is God's.'' On the other hand, many of Jesus' sayings are suggestive figures and brief comparisons: thus they have in fact a narrative character. See, for example, Matt. 5:13: ''You are the salt of the earth; now if the salt loses its strength, wherewith shall it be salted? It is no longer good for anything but to be thrown out and to be trodden under foot by people.'' To the question, ''Who is my neighbor?'' Jesus answers in Luke 10:25-37 with a narrative example: ''A certain man went down from Jerusalem to Jericho.''

The narratives about Jesus and his words are also so closely joined together because in Jesus' own conduct, word and deed were closely joined. A. N. Wilder correctly remarks: "Here it is important to make clear what the formative element is in many of the smallest units of the early Christian literature. We speak of it as the Good News. But it is Good News of a total and ultimate kind, and not only recited but effectively and dynamically demonstrated. . . . It determines the basic speech-mode of Christianity which is that of a story, and therefore the Gospel anecdotes, but, of course, especially the Gospels." [8]

The tradition was first of all oral tradition. Jesus himself *preached,* and he preached in such a way that his words could be remembered.[9] His discourse was of a narrative, pictorial kind, and the tradition preserved that character. I quote Wilder again: "Oral speech is where it all began. Jesus and his first followers used the different modes of language which we know as a dialogue, story and poem, well before it occurred to anyone to set anything down on papyrus, leather, or tablet. Even when they did come to write we can overhear the living voices, speaking and praising. This kind of writing is very close to speech." [10] Therefore even after so many centuries the reader still is constantly being addressed, summoned to a face-to-face encounter. "The new utterance of the Gospel can never settle comfortably into any fixtures of formula or print or book, though with new cultural situations it can shape these also in a way to safeguard the immediacies of faith." [11]

The dialogue is aimed at the heart of the one addressed, but also to the hearts of those to whom the story of the dialogue is handed down. It takes place in the context of the dialogue between heaven and earth.[12]

The *stories* are actually miniature gospels, highly diverse, just as the hearers (and now the readers) are also highly diverse. One should note the sermons in Acts which are plainly narrative, and the narrative construction of the early confessions of faith such as I Tim. 3:16 and Phil. 2:5-11. On this, Wilder says: "When the Christian in any time or place confesses his faith, his confession turns into a narrative." [13] With the parables it is striking that on the one hand traditional figures are used (for example, that of the vineyard, of the king, the judgment, etc.), part of them also from the sphere of apocalyptic thought, and that on the other hand they clearly depict ordinary, everyday situations (in which ordinary as well as extraordinary things happen). Wilder places great emphasis on this last element. Thus directly, concretely, secularly, Jesus (as a layman) brought the gospel. [14]

With reference to the poetic passages it is proper to point to very familiar Old Testament examples (e.g., Exod. 15, Gen. 49, Deut. 32, Judg. 5, I Sam. 2, and the Psalms) and to approximately contemporary parallels also (e. g., in the psalms of Solomon and the hymns of Qumran). The New Testament knows only a few genuine hymns (Luke 1); we do find all sorts of hymnic passages in the Epistles (see, for example, Eph. 5:14; I Tim. 3:16) and poetic prose as well. The significance of this is indicated by Wilder in the sentence which is characteristic of him: "When the dumb are cured in Scripture they not only speak but sing; just as when the crippled are healed they not only walk but leap." [15]

The Function of Pictorial and Narrative Language

It will not surprise us that in his closing chapter[16] Wilder places heavy emphasis on the pictorial, symbolic, and mythical character of the language employed in the New Testament. Herein it is in agreement with the Old Testament. The new faith experience of the Christians reshaped old, existing images and created new ones (one should think, for example, of the Apocalypse of John!). We detect a peculiar duality in the attitude toward picture

92

and myth. On the one hand we find clearly in the New Testament (and in the Old) demythologizing and doing away with images, and on the other hand people there themselves speak of God's relationship with men in figurative, symbolic, or narrative terms. They could not do otherwise. "The Gospel did, indeed, combat the myth of the time, but it was also a myth-making movement. One cannot say which came first, the eschatological sense of being at the embattled frontier between an old and a new world, or the imagery and *mythos* that reflected the experience and made it meaningful." [17] Therefore any demythologizing, although indispensable whenever the myth is used by literal minds and thus is misjudged as to its true intention, is doomed in advance to failure. How shall one ever be able to reproduce in argumentation what can be evoked with a picture or illustrated in a story?

When demythologizing is directed against literalism or against dogmatic objectifying and secularizing of Christian faith and its images, we cannot but approve its aim. Faith should not be confused with acceptance of God's dealings taken as blueprints for belief, let alone credulity. But demythologizing fails to do justice to the meaning and truth in the imagery. . . . Transposition of the myth into provisional discursive or existential analogies is desirable provided it be recognized that every such formulation is a poor surrogate and must always again appeal back to the original. [18]

Two aspects of the narrative, figurative language in the early Christian tradition need to be brought out here.

In the first place, it must be noted that by our standards people very freely handled the narrative material which was available to them. The parable of the wicked tenants in Mark 12:1-12 has a clear Christological point: one should note the expression "beloved son" in verse 6, the question in verses 10-11, and the context (this is immediately preceded by the story of the inquiry about Jesus' authority in 11:27-33). In Matthew (21:33-46), the

93

parable clearly stands in a salvation history connection: Israel rejects the one sent by God, and the Christian community accepts him. This is indicated by the alterations made by Matthew in the narrative and particularly in its setting (see especially vss. 41a and 43), as well as by the context in which Matthew places the parable: it is preceded by the parable of the two sons (21:28-32) and followed by that of the wedding feast (22:1-14), both of which have the same point. It is not a simple matter to discover in what form and with what aim Jesus spoke this parable![19] In any case it is evident that people freely altered sayings of Jesus and adapted them to the situation in which the writer lived.

An entirely different example is the story preserved in Matt. 9:27-31 of the healing of the two blind men, an evident doublet of Matt. 20:29-34 (parallels in Mark 10:46-52; Luke 18:35-43). Why does Matthew tell this story twice, or why does he in any case tell two stories so closely resembling each other? In chapters 8 and 9 he brings together a number of miracle stories, with an eye to Jesus' answer to John the Baptist related in 11:5. There reference is made, among other things, to the fact that blind people are receiving their sight; Matthew appropriates a story about the healing of a blind person which appears just after this in the Gospel of Mark which he is using, alters it, and fits it in here; later he gives it again, in a somewhat different form, when he encounters it anew, following the order of Mark.[20]

In the Gospel of Mark it is striking how after the story of the feeding of the five thousand (Mark 6:32-44) there follows, in Mark 8:1-10, the feeding of the four thousand.[21] In any case, with him these stories function within a theological framework. At the first feeding, twelve basketsful are left over (an allusion to Israel?), and at the second, seven (an allusion to the nations? cf. Acts 6:3).[22] Moreover, the second feeding is clearly placed within the context of a journey of Jesus outside the Jewish territory (7:24, 31; 8:10).[23] Here is put into practice what is suggested in the conversation with the Syro-Phoenician woman: the children ought to be satisfied first, and then the dogs (Mark 7:24-30).[24] Did Mark know two stories (and in that case did a doubling occur in an earlier stage of the tradition?), or did Mark himself create two versions of one story? Thus in this example just as in the preceding one we apparently have to do with an obvious case of a shaping of a new story (by Mark, or in an earlier stage of the tradition) after the analogy of available material. This proves again how free people were with respect to what was given to them by the past, but at the same time how naturally people clothed their message in narrative form.

In the second place it needs to be indicated here once again that the tradition handed down in the New Testament shows a great diversity in its figurative and narrative language, not only because it deals with various situations and various persons, but also because it comprehends that the matter being treated, the God of whom it speaks, and the man Jesus in whom he is revealed, cannot be contained in one word, one story, one image. There are many parables of the kingdom of God. It has already been noted above[25] that God is the Father and the judge and the husbandman and the king, and so on. And again he is always these in a different way from the way a man would be any one of them. We read it and are amazed. He shatters our images and transcends them, while we yet may maintain a very personal relationship to him. Indeed, precisely because he is thus different, the personal relationship is for us both fundamental and unique, the one pearl for which we may sell all that we possess (Matt. 13:45).

Theology as Narrative

A simple, credulous retelling from one generation to another, consciously and unconsciously alluding to the questions of our own time and our own situation, is impossible for us. As children of our time we cannot detach ourselves from the modern historical critical approach to the past, from the philosophical tradition of Europe, and from the scientific, technical way of viewing the world.

The modern historical critical approach also analyzes the tradition. The present chapter is a modest contribution to this analysis, which inquires after the earlier and later stages in the tradition, investigates the influence of the *Sitz im Leben* on what is handed down, and tries (though very cautiously) also to reach conclusions about what is authentic and what is not authentic. It respects *the role of the subject* in the tradition, lets heavy stress be placed on *the time-bound character and particularity produced by the milieu,* and therewith as a matter of course underscores *the diversity* in the stance and the formulation of faith within the early church.

The discovery of the important role which the subject played led, with Bultmann, to giving a central position to the existential interpretation. This, however, was coupled with a very heavy emphasis on the individual experience, on the inward aspects, and on the present.[26] Hence with Bultmann theology is reduced to a philosophical theological analysis of man in his relationship to God[27]; there is no place for narrative. It is entirely different with Paul van Buren. Speaking of the new discernment and the commitment that issues from it, he writes: "the new discernment and its accompanying commitment to a way of life is experienced as a response. This perspective arises in connection with hearing the Gospel concerning Jesus of Nazareth and it looks back to him continually as its historical point of orientation. To affirm the Gospel is to express this historical perspective."[28]

Here there remains a place for the narrative; full emphasis is rightly placed on the discernment (corresponding to faith in the traditional historical perspectives) and on the commitment (and thus on the unity of faith and life; compare Wilder's emphasis on the unity of word and deed in Jesus), but in the narrative God is at most present incognito. Can we (while taking fully seriously what was said at the beginning of this section) also now still speak about God and about Jesus in narratives which are concrete, human, secular through and through, and thus plainly translate a view of man and the world and history, and in so doing still provide room for the dynamic power of the "Name"? Can we retell the story about Jesus that was told to us, in such a way that others discover and encounter the Father in him (John 14:9), again praise his name, and preach in a new language? And so that we, moreover, come to an unequivocal response indeed (commitment)?

We can strive to retell the old stories. But then this presupposes that, fully honoring the historical investigation, we shall try to identify with the original narrator(s) and let it be seen how the narrative functioned in the past. Further, we shall then let the narrative do its work in its own way.

We can strive, extending the line already present in the earliest tradition, to actualize the stories, with due regard, naturally, for the narrative form. This demands a thorough analysis of our own situation, a keen theological insight, and a creative ability. In addition, we, schooled in historical thinking, will actualize them in a way different from that which was followed in the tradition before us.

We can also tell new stories; that is to say, with a vision that is sharpened by what has been handed down to us and by the historical analysis of it, we can draw connecting lines between then and now. This is risky business, but talking about God is always risky; in doing this, orientation to Jesus remains essential.[29] In an analogous way we can also try to tell new parables.

The telling of any story, however, will remain unbelievable if the creative word is not coupled with the creative deed. In every-

97

thing inspiration by the Holy Spirit is and remains essential. Of him it is said in John 16:13-15: "But when the Spirit of truth comes, he will initiate you into the whole truth. He does not speak on his own authority, but hands on what he hears and announces what is going to happen. Thus he gives me the honor that belongs to me; for he has received from me all that he will be saying to you. And I have received it all from the Father."

VII

Communication in Word and in Silence

Introduction

In the preceding chapters the subject of speaking has come up again and again: the first Christians' speaking about Jesus, and contemporary Christians' speaking about Jesus and about God.[1] In the sixth chapter special emphasis was placed on the dynamic, appealing character of the speech of Jesus himself and of his first disciples, and on the connection between speaking and acting with Jesus and his people.

It will be useful in this chapter to deal with the question of the connection between speech and silence in our relationship with God and in handing on the proclamation of and about Jesus. Silence can guard our speech against degeneration into drivel. In order really to speak sensibly about Jesus and God we need also to be able to be silent.

Silence and Speech

Silence is the absence of speech or noise (Concise Oxford Dictionary). On the part of man this silence is due to abstention from speech; he keeps silent. Silence is a deliberate human act, because man is in a position to choose between silence and speaking. Therefore it is no use stating explicitly that a person is silent unless he could normally have been speaking in the circumstances. If we say that John was reading silently in his study during the whole afternoon, the word "silently" is superfluous, unless John is known to be in the habit of humming or singing during his work or of making a lot of noise. We cannot begin a conversation when we are alone, so it is unnecessary to state that we keep silent under these circumstances. And in the case of John's habit of humming we mention his silence only because that humming or singing has usually been heard by other people in the house.

Speaking presupposes and creates a relation between two or more people; it is a communicative act. In the same way keeping silence, presupposing the alternative of speaking, is essentially communicative.

Just as there is a difference between speaking and speaking, there is a difference between silence and silence. Moreover, the quality of speech conditions the quality of silence and vice versa. Speech may be no more than chatter, twaddle, empty talk. It may be a flood of words to avoid silence, like music on the radio which is not even noticed by those who are supposed to be listening to it. Similarly silence may be no more than emptiness, a gap in our noise; usually empty talk creates an empty silence and it is very difficult to speak meaningful words after a meaningless silence. But if a conversation is really an exchange of our deepest thoughts and brings about understanding, real communication, and even fellowship, silence may be a means of intensified communication and equally meaningful as words, or even more meaningful. On the other hand: if silence is born out of mutual understanding and fellowship, even simple words may be full of meaning.

This leads to the conclusion that speech and silence are important and interrelated elements within the total process of communication between men. Communication is not only a matter of words or of the deliberate or natural abstention from words—it is also a matter of our various senses, it is an encounter from man to

100

man and not an exclusively spiritual event. But as man is endowed with reason, thought and speech are essential means of communication for him.

The interrelation between speech and silence is very well illustrated in a story by the German author Heinrich Böll called "Doktor Murkes gesammeltes Schweigen" ("Murke's Collected Silences").[2]

Dr. Murke is a brilliant young psychologist who works for a broadcasting station. He receives the assignment to cut the word God out of the tapes of two half-hour talks given by a scholarly and prolific author of essays on religious, philosophical, and cultural subjects named Bur-Malottke. Overnight this Bur-Malottke has come to the conclusion that he can no longer take the responsibility for the word God used in the two lectures which he has had recorded, and he wants to replace it with the expression "that higher Being Whom we revere."

This replacement, however, gives rise to a number of serious problems, because this new expression varies, in German, according to the case in which it is used. It is a trying morning—for Dr. Murke, who has to sort out all the occurrences of "God" according to the various cases (there turn out to be twenty-seven altogether), and for Bur-Malottke, who has to say "that higher Being Whom we revere" twenty-seven times, with the appropriate grammatical adjustments. Dr. Murke collects the twenty-seven pieces of tape with "God" in a cigarette box, reports to the head of his department, and tells him that he simply cannot stand hearing Bur-Malottke any more. His superior sympathizes with him and tells how in his younger days he was cured of Nazism after listening to a four-hour speech by Hitler three times in order to be able to shorten it by three minutes. During this conversation, however, he discovers another little box with pieces of tape in Murke's desk. It turns out to contain silence. Dr. Murke collects silence.

101

The quality of this silence is aptly illustrated in the second part of the story which describes how Murke is waiting at home for the telephone call from the studio telling him that he can take the afternoon off to go to the movies with his girl friend.

Dr. Murke and the girl sit silently in his room, a turning tape recorder between them. Not a word was spoken, no sound was heard. One could have taken the girl for a mannikin, so beautiful and so mute was she.

"I can't stand it," said the girl suddenly, "I can't stand it, it's inhuman, what you want me to do. There are some men who expect a girl to do immoral things, but it seems to me that what you are asking me to do is even more immoral than the things other men expect a girl to do."

Murke sighed. "Oh hell," he said, "Rina dear, now I've got to cut all that out; do be sensible, be a good girl and put just five more minutes' silence on the tape" (p. 145).

Bur-Malottke's words were empty, and he was not the only speaker on the department's tapes with whom that was the case. We can understand Dr. Murke's longing for silence. But the very fact that he could cut out the pieces of silent tape shows that this silence was empty too. If the short periods of silence had been meaningful within the context of a meaningful speech Dr. Murke could not have removed them without doing serious damage to the whole.

Empty speech and empty silence have, in fact, dehumanized Dr. Murke and disturbed his relations with his fellowmen. When he is together with an attractive girl he asks the girl to be silent not *with,* but *for* him. He says "I have your silence in the original and on tape, that's terrific" (p. 146), without realizing that this silence too is empty, inhuman, immoral because there is no real communication between this girl and himself either in speaking or in silence. Silence and words are both meaningless. The girl's name is only mentioned in passing; she is almost anonymous—she was "pretty and silent enough," Böll tells us, "for a photographer's model."

But if there had been real communication and fellowship between these two, could their joint silence (not the girl's own silence) have kept its meaning after having been recorded on the tape? Dr. Murke dehumanized his contact with the girl (and she felt it) by the very fact that he thought that he could isolate her individual silence and put this silence, taken out of its original human context, on a tape. Because his sense of real human communication was disturbed, Dr. Murke did not realize how he denatured silence by collecting pieces of silent tape.

Man as a Being Who Speaks and Keeps Silent

Real communication, true fellowship between men, presupposes an exchange of thoughts and words as well as silence. An effective exchange of thoughts requires careful listening. Listening is an art—it waits for the other's words, and it elicits the good, the true words. The attentive listener helps the speaker to find the words he wants to find and thereby helps to clarify his thoughts. The alternation of listening and speaking is essential for a good conversation.

It should be emphasized, I think, that silence, though it is essential for a true functioning of speech and for communication among men, is not preferable to speech. A proper evaluation of the meaning of silence should not lead to an underestimation of the use of words. Man is man because he is able to speak, to express his thoughts, and to convey them to others. Man is a logical being, a *zoön logikon*. "Logos" in Greek means "word" and "discourse" as well as thought.

Man speaks, and in speaking he does not only express his thoughts, he also clarifies them. Thought and word cannot be separated, no more than spirit and body. Everyone who has

103

experience in teaching knows that the necessity of conveying one's thoughts by means of words compels one to express them very clearly, and often it is this compulsion which clarifies one's own thoughts. At the same time, of course, it is not only important how we say it, but also how we are ourselves, as teachers. Speech is not everything, but it is essential in human communication and in individual self-expression. Only within the context of meaningful speech can silence be meaningful.

Because words cannot express and convey everything, speaking needs silence; but if we do not struggle with mind and soul to find the right words and discover by trial and error the limitations of our words, we shall not discover the necessity and the value of silence—and the necessity of finding other ways of expression and of trying to find other words after and out of that silence. The scientist formulates a theory, but will soon discover its limitations. A poet will write a poem because he feels an inner need to write it, but is dissatisfied with the poem and with himself as soon as he has finished it. We write a letter to someone we know very well, to express our joy or our sorrow, but we tear it to pieces because we seem not to be able to find the right words. But the scientist will try to find a new formula, the poet will write another poem, and we know we have to write another letter and so begin again.

Silence and Silence

Words may hurt people; speech is one of the sharpest weapons in the struggle between man and man. In our times we realize how destructive the suggestive force of words can be, confronted as we have been and still are with propaganda and mass hysteria.

But silence also has its demonic side. Keeping silent may have something uncanny about it. "Please, do say something," we cry, because this silence makes us feel uncomfortable. We can ignore a person completely and refuse to talk to him because we cannot stand him or because there is an unresolved conflict between us. Our silence may be as hard as stone and as cold as ice; it may have something of the atmosphere of death around it. We may be silent as the grave, and indeed, we do not speak if we are confronted by death. Also in this respect silence in itself is not preferable to speech. When James says of our tongue, "We use it to sing the praises of our Lord and Father, and we use it to invoke curses upon our fellow-men who are made in God's likeness. Out of the same mouth come praises and curses. My brothers, this should not be so" (James 3:9-10, NEB), the same could have been said of silence.

A good example of the negative power of silence is found in Vercors' story "Le silence de la mer" ("The silence of the sea") which became a best seller in the Netherlands after the war. It is the story of a Frenchman and his niece who receive a German officer, billeted in their house, with a correct but icy silence. In the beginning they feel that their silence is right and dignified, but gradually it becomes a burden. The German turns out to be a "good" German who longs and works for a better understanding between France and Germany and sees Germany's faults very clearly. Evening after evening he speaks about his ideals and his concerns without ever getting any response. In the end the German officer volunteers for service on the Russian front—his German friends laugh about his ideals, and his French hosts do not answer him. At their last meeting he hears—for the first time and for the last—"please, come in, sir" and "au revoir." The next morning, at breakfast, the Frenchman and his niece sit silently opposite one another. "She served the breakfast silently, we drank silently. Outside a pale sun shone through the morning mist. I had the feeling that it was very cold."

Of course, we all know that silence need not be hard and cold. It need not have the atmosphere of death around it but, on the contrary, can create an atmosphere of light and life. When there is real fellowship between people, half a word, a hint, will be sufficient, and an eloquent silence will give expression to all that is felt and shared, a common life of love and understanding. But it is good to bear in mind the other, demonic, possibilities of silence as well.

Speaking About God and Keeping Silent

Man's speech is not only a means of communication with his fellowmen, but he also speaks to and about God. He may also be silent about God and towards God. But here too, speech and silence are interrelated, and silence is not essentially preferable to speech. Words about God may be meaningless, and silent worship may be empty. Words may be felt to be inspired by God and speak to the condition of the community present, and silence may be filled by the presence of God. As Rufus M. Jones said: "[The early Friends] made the discovery that silence is one of the best preparations for communion [with God] and for the reception of inspiration and guidance. Silence itself, of course, has no magic. It may be sheer emptiness, absence of words or noise or music. It may be an occasion for slumber, or it may be a dead form. But it may be an intensified pause, a vitalized hush, a creative quiet, an actual moment of mutual and reciprocal correspondence with God. The actual meeting of man with God and God with man is the very crown and culmination of what we can do with our human life here on earth." [3]

Communication between man and God cannot be effected by man himself; it is brought about by God, conferred by God. To make our words powerful and true to God's intentions we need the help of his Holy Spirit; and that same Spirit is needed to make our silence into a real worshiping silence out of which a true testimony can be born.

106

In a silent meeting for worship, such as the Quakers have, words and silence condition each other. At the same time our communication with one another—also on the purely human level, outside the meeting for worship—conditions our communion with God just as a new sense of fellowship and of mutual responsibility can grow out of our communion with God. I John 4:7-21 does not leave any doubt about this.

Christianity is the religion of the Word, spoken by God through the ages, and become man in Jesus of Nazareth. All God has to say was said in Jesus. His message was not just a matter of human words—it was the message of a human life. The witness of Christians, which is centered upon this man sent by God and springs from this source, can never be a matter of words only—it is a witness of human lives. "My children, love must not be a matter of words or talk, it must be genuine, and show itself in action" (I John 3:18, NEB). But this message cannot and need not be given without words. Communication without words would be subhuman, even inhuman; speaking about God in words is always inadequate and therefore a superhuman task, but "do not worry about what you are to say; when the time comes, the words you need will be given to you: for it is not you who will be speaking; it will be the Spirit of your Father speaking in you" (Matt. 10:19-20, NEB). To be silent before God and to give concrete form to our words in deeds of love is just as impossible a task—which can only be accomplished, and is accomplished, thank God, through the power of the Spirit.

In the belief that the message about Jesus Christ is always new, Christianity has always struggled to find new words to convey this message, and it has experimented to find new forms of Christian community life. In many fields Quakers have been and are pioneers in their ministry of love, in their exploration of new and useful tasks in a world of need, and in their attempts at furthering reconciliation between men. They have given and are giving

useful service to mankind and to their fellow Christians by show-
ing how Christians may live for others.

It appears not unreasonable, however, to say that the Quakers
have paid rather less attention to the urgent task of rewording the
Christian message, the struggle to find new expressions which
may answer the questions of men in the various parts of a rapidly
changing world. It would be a good thing if the Quakers with their
experience of living silence would help to discover the possibilities of a new living Christian speech and to coin a new
language suitable to convey the message about Jesus Christ to our
world. Their own silent worship would benefit from this intensive
occupation with the verbal witness, and both the other Christian
communities and the Society of Friends would have occasion to
be very grateful for this joint activity.

The last part of Heinrich Böll's "Doktor Murkes gesammeltes
Schweigen" shows the difficulties connected with religious
speech. At the same moment that Dr. Murke and Rina leave to go
to the movies, an assistant producer is listening to the play which
is to be broadcast that evening, and he is not satisfied with the end
of it. An atheist is speaking in a large, empty, resounding church,
asking: "Who will remember me when I have become the prey of
worms? Who will wait for me when I have turned to dust?" There
are twelve such questions, each spoken a little louder than the
preceding one. Of course, the atheist does not receive any answer;
after each question there is absolute silence.

The producer and the technician assisting him come to the
conclusion that there is far too much silence in it and look for a
solution. Suddenly the technician remembers the twenty-seven
words "God" cut out of that morning's lectures, and with the
author's permission twelve pieces of tape from Bur-Malottke's
lectures are used to fill up the gaps of silence in the play. They are
admirably suited for the purpose because they were spoken in an
ordinary room free of the resonance of the church and for this

108

reason create the impression of coming from a totally different place.

" 'It's a simple matter, of course,' said the technician, 'to cut out the silence and stick in God twelve times'" (p. 148). Of course it was not as simple as he thought. In this case silence was right, and the word "God" was not, because it did not give a real answer to the atheist's question. Better a silence charged with scorn, despair, or anxious expectation than a word which is thrown in somewhat carelessly, especially if this word is "God."

What should a Christian do, if he hears such questions? He should start by joining in the silence out of sympathy with the atheist's questions because he recognizes his own problems in them. He should try to speak later on, perhaps at the second or third meeting, because he cannot keep silent but has to bear witness to the answers which he has received himself. He should speak, hesitatingly, modestly, and above all carefully, trying to remain in real communication with the atheist, attempting to be true to that man's views and to his own. He should speak out of the silence which he shares with the other man, the silence with which everyone is confronted who asks the central questions of life—but he is not allowed to keep silent. It is not his task to convince the other, even less to be more clever than the other, but he is asked to be a witness to God's love with his whole life, including his words and his silence.

VIII

To Love
as God Loves

Introduction

"We live in a strange no-man's-land between rigid rules and loose morals. The rigid rules of the traditional civic Christian morality no longer have much to say to us, and the loose morals of an age obsessed with possessions, violence, and sex inspire no one to responsible actions."[1] J. de Graaf said this in his essay "Het ethos van de Brief van Jakobus en onze hedendaagse ethische vragen" ("The ethos of the Epistle of James and our contemporary ethical issues") in the recent little Eltheto book *Geloven met je handen* ("Believe with your hands").[2] It is in this no-man's-land that the ethicists operate; even Christian ethicists, who (in de Graaf's terminology) inquire how the ethos that comes to light in the writings of the New Testament can have an inspiring impact upon the actions of Christians (and non-Christians) in our time.

Some of these Christian ethicists say to us that one must venture into the no-man's-land with love as the only compass —love in the sense of Christian *agape*. The territory has not been mapped[3]; there are no signposts to be found, and there are few landmarks. Of course we need to proceed with due caution and reflection; we must not be so stupid as the young woman just married who did not want to look at a cookbook and wanted to bake a cake for her husband guided only by her love for him.[4] Of course we must let ourselves be guided by our own experience and that of others in other areas and at other times, but in the last analysis we shall always have to decide *ad hoc,* and nothing is prescribed except the deliberate use of the compass, love.

"Nothing Prescribed—Except Love": J. A. T. Robinson places this heading over one of the sections in his sixth chapter on the new morality in his *Honest to God.*[5] "Love Is the Only Norm" is the title of the fourth chapter of Joseph Fletcher's *Situation Ethics*. This does not mean that commandments, rules, norms are finished; in his *Christian Morals Today,*[6] J. A. T. Robinson expressly places the so-called new morality not in opposition to the old but alongside it, and Joseph Fletcher really does give the law a place, though a subordinate one: "We follow law, *if at all,* for love's sake, we do not love for law's sake."[7] Those who recommend love as the only ultimate norm of Christian action, however, do set themselves unequivocally against any and all legalism. They are against antinomianism, too (even though it were only because they themselves have been charged with antinomianism[8]); but because in recent times legalism has exerted a much greater influence in civil and Christian circles in Western Europe and North America, those who adhere to situation ethics address themselves to all those who take as their starting point the universally valid commandments which ought to be applied, and therefore *are* applicable as well, in all situations. To let Fletcher speak once more: "Christian ethics or moral theology is not a scheme of living according to a code, but a continuous effort to relate love to a world of relativities through a casuistry obedient to love; its constant task is to work out the strategy and tactics of love, for Christ's sake."[9]

Now there is no other writing or group of writings in the New Testament in which so much is said about love and loving as in the Epistles of John. Of the 141 places where the verb appears in

111

the New Testament, we find 31 (22 percent) in the Epistles of John, while the epistles comprise only 12 of the 657 pages (i.e., 1.8 percent) of Nestle's edition of the Greek text. As for the substantive: in the Epistles of John we find *agape* 21 times, and 116 times in the entire New Testament: that is, 18 percent of the cases appear in 1.8 percent of the text.[10] These proportions are not even remotely approached by any other writing in the New Testament.[11] Now of course the significance of words for a particular author cannot be measured by the number of times that he uses them, but the figures just cited in any case still point in a definite direction, and a closer examination of the content of the epistles shows that love and loving indeed play a very important role in the argument.

Thus it is all the more reasonable to explore what is said about *agape* in this group of writings because, generally speaking, the attention of Christian ethicists is directed more to the Sermon on the Mount and other radical sayings of Jesus on the one hand and to Pauline statements about the relation of law and gospel on the other hand than to the ethical expressions in the Gospel and the Epistles of John.[12] My present study is historically and exegetically oriented; in the following pages, the main concern is an answer to the question of how the author of the Epistles of John reacts to the situation in which he finds himself and how he speaks of love in that context. The results of this study have been, for me at least, surprising; they can perhaps be inspiring and authoritative for Christians of these times. In what measure and in what way this is the case is not for the exegete to decide. Neither the scientific approach to the New Testament nor ethics is served by discussions under the title, "What the Bible says about . . . ," like those that claim to derive rules and insights that are suitable for the present day from rules and insights in the diverse collection of books that has come down to us as Bible. It is much more fruitful carefully to investigate a part of the Bible historically, in our case the Epistles of John, so that later the ethicist, who builds upon the conclusions reached by exegesis with full and due regard for the great difference in the situation, can indicate to what extent what was said then can be relevant for the present. What has been said in this introduction thus has been motivation for a historical and exegetical investigation which remains concentrated on the past; I do hope that it will inspire others to go further, for example in the style of the above-named essay by de Graaf in the Eltheto booklet.

The Plan of the Discussion

In what follows, the following four questions come in for primary consideration. The first question is: In what situation is the author writing and to whom is he addressing himself? It will appear that he is dealing with people who consider themselves highly spiritual, and from their spiritual status they deduce that the commandments that are binding on ordinary mortals do not apply to them. Thus after this issue is treated, attention must be given to the question of how the author sees the relationship between following God's commandments and loving, between righteousness and love. The third question is that of the relationship between the love of God (and of Christ) for man and the love of man for his brother. Finally, it will appear necessary explicitly to dwell on the question of who, according to these epistles, is regarded as brother. Does the word refer to fellow Christians or to fellowmen?

The study is focused primarily on the First Epistle of John; the Second Epistle gives only a brief summary of what is important in the first and then devotes two verses (5 and 6) to love without saying anything new. In the Third Epistle the verb and the noun each appear once (in vss. 1 and 6 respectively), without any special emphasis being placed on them. The central pericope in I

113

John is 4:7-21, to which 5:1-4 can be added. In keeping with the peculiar style of argumentation in this epistle—which is rightly characterized by C. H. Dodd as spiral[13]—the subject is, however, already earlier treated, though only in a preliminary way, in 2:7-11 (with 2:5-6 as preamble and 2:15 as conclusion) and in 3:10-18 (with 3:23).

The Author and His Opponents

The First and Second Epistles of John are addressed to a community or group of communities to warn them against preachers who in the eyes of the author are proclaiming a false doctrine and are leading a wrong life. It is the latter, the life, that the author discusses rather than the former. Three times in 1:5-10 we find the expression, "If we say that" (vss. 6, 8, 10), and similarly in 2:3-11 three times the expression, "Whoever says that" (vss. 4, 6, 9). It is very likely that the author here is citing and judging claims of his adversaries.

What are these people saying and what is the author's charge against them?[14]

1:6: "If we claim to share in his life, while our ways are dark, we are lying with both words and deeds."

1:8: "If we claim to be without sin, we are deluding ourselves, and the truth does not dwell in us."

1:10: "If we say that we have not committed any sin, we make him out a liar; then his word does not dwell in us."

2:4: "Whoever says, 'I know him,' but does not heed his commandments is a liar; the truth does not dwell in any such person."

2:6: "Anyone who claims communion with God must live as Christ lived."

2:9: "Anyone who says that he is in the light but hates his brother is still in the darkness."

114

The adversaries evidently are laying claim to a special insight into the divine mysteries, to a life in close communion with God. They know God (2:4), abide in him (2:6), are in the light (2:9), have fellowship with him (also translated as "have a share in his life," [1:6]), and claim to be without sin (1:8, 10). These claims are lies, says the writer of I John; these people are not what they pretend to be, their lives are lies, because they are walking in darkness (1:6; 2:9), they hate their brothers (2:9), and they disregard God's commandments (2:4). The criterion for a life such as they claim to live is a manner of life that corresponds to that of Jesus Christ (2:6). No one is sinless by his own power and safeguarded against the possibility of sinning, though we may trust in the forgiveness and atonement bestowed by God in Jesus (1:7,9; 2:1-2; 4:10).

The author places heavy emphasis on heeding and thus living according to God's commandments, as these are revealed and lived in Jesus (see, in addition to 2:6, also 3:3, 7, 16). And this life of Jesus is indissolubly bound up with his death, which has wrought the forgiveness and atonement for us. In 3:16 we read: "We have learned from Christ what love is: he has given his life for us. Thus we are obliged also to give our lives for our brothers." This is not only an important ethical position, but also a central point of faith. Here it is presupposed that Jesus has lived a real life, endured real sufferings, and that we may believe not only in the exemplary character of his sacrifice, but also in the salvation that is bestowed on us therein.

The false teachers—this appears from the combatting of their beliefs in 2:18-27; 4:1-6; 5:5-8; and II John 7-9—have denied Jesus' humanity and his crucifixion. At least the author thus portrays their position. Thereby these adversaries have cut themselves off from the source of all life; they do not know God at all, they know nothing of God's forgiveness, they do not take God's commandments seriously, they do not know what love really is,

115

and this then appears from the fact that they do not love their brothers. According to 2:19, these adversaries have separated themselves from the church(es) to whom the author is writing. This was even unavoidable: they did not belong there, for they are not children of God but the devil's brood. They have passed over from the kingdom of light to the domain of darkness; the author thinks in sharply dualistic terms (see especially 3:4-10 and 4:1-6).

What is needed is a reorientation to the basic facts of the Christian proclamation; according to 1:1-4, the author insists on this, in a reorientation to the Christian tradition which goes back to the eyewitnesses, who assure us that in Jesus the Life really is revealed. Anyone who seeks for light, truth, knowledge, communion with God, and so forth in any other way, and pretends to possess them, is lying—in his doctrine and in his life. For the author of I John, however, tradition is not the management of a legacy, but a process in which what has been entrusted to the community can *continue* to work. This is why on the one hand he goes back to the traditional terminology (for example, in 1:7b, 9; 2:1, 18; 3:10; 4:10; 5:1, etc.), but on the other hand goes further and arrives at new formulations in the dialogue with the adversaries.

Of course we must take account of the fact that he may have distorted the opinions of his opponents; he fights them with passion as antichrists, and for him the truth is at stake. Hence it is not easy to reconstruct, out of the dispute, a clear picture of what the opponents themselves positively claimed. But it is not too venturesome to assume that here we have to do with people who are spiritual fanatics, who regarded themselves already as participants in the present in the kingdom of the Spirit and therefore looked down on and separated themselves from those who were less gifted; people who thought that for them God's commandments no longer were in force and that they, living by the Spirit, could make their decisions *ad hoc;* people who in dogmatic

116

respects were of the opinion that Christ as the first and exemplary spiritual man could not have had anything to do with the flesh, and for this reason saw and venerated the Son of God as a purely spiritual being.

One can say that they, along with all of early Christianity living in the tension between the "not yet" and "already," the salvation and judgment yet to be expected *and* what is already realized in Jesus Christ and his community, stake everything on the "now, already." Thereby they have drawn the future to themselves, have lost the tie with the past, and have wrongly interpreted the present; and thereby they have come to float above the earth and have lost sight of their brothers insofar as the latter are not elevated above the world along with them.

Over against these, the author of I John remains with both feet on the ground—he knows very well the "not yet," he still lives simply in the time of testing before the end (see, for example, 2:18) and knows of the judgment that is coming (see, for example, 2:28-3:3; 4:17); he knows the temptations that threaten now to bring people to apostasy (see, for example, 2:15-17); he knows that the main thing is to remain steadfast and to show oneself to be faithful[15]; and he is persuaded that one can do this only if one is oriented to what is handed down in the reliable, authoritative tradition with reference to what God has done, given, and commanded in Jesus. Of course the "already" is of great importance to the author: "We have passed from death to life; we know this because we love our brothers" (3:14), but he places the "already" between the "once" and the "not yet" and is of the opinion that only thus is the "already" rightly understood.

Love and Commandment

In opposition to the spiritual antinomianism of his adversaries[16] the author of I John places great emphasis on the keeping of the concrete commandments. Characteristic is the argument of 2:3-11. First of all, it is stated that "knowing God" is indissolubly bound up with "keeping his commandments" (2:3-4). From this the conclusion is drawn: "But in a man who is obedient to God's word, his love actually reaches its perfection" (2:5). The second half of this verse will be discussed in the next section; at this point I wish to fix attention on the fact that the author passes over from "the commandments" to "the word," and only once in 2:7 to speak of "the commandment," which again is defined as "the word which you have heard from the beginning." That one commandment is the old one "that you have always had" (2:7)[17]; that is to say, it belongs to the original deposit of the Christian preaching; reference is made to the statement which is handed down in John 13:34 as a saying of Jesus: "A new commandment I give to you, that you love another; as I have loved you, that you also love one another." The fact that what is meant here is actually a reference to the tradition recorded in John 13:34 appears from what follows. It is no new commandment, says the author, you have had it all along, and yet it is a new commandment because "the darkness is passing away and the true light is already shining" (2:8). What was commanded then and still is commanded is now already in the process of being realized in a surprisingly new fashion.

Thus the commandments are summed up in the one new old commandment; they are comprehended in the message which is being proclaimed from God. This one commandment is the commandment of love for one's brother; this appears in 2:9-11 and is also said in so many words in 4:21: "This commandment then we also have received from him: whoever loves God must love his brother also." This love is indissolubly bound up with faith; here one should note especially 3:22-24. In verses 22 and 24 the author speaks of keeping God's commandments as an aspect of the inward bond between man and God, and then in verse 23 we read:

118

"And this is his commandment, to believe in his Son Jesus Christ and to love one another as he has commanded us." Thus faith also, which may be directed to the message, is commanded just as love, which is directed to the love of God proclaimed in the message, is commanded.[18]

What now does the expression "God's commandment(s)" specifically include? In the first place it has to do with what is commanded by God in Jesus Christ; it is evident that the "from the beginning" in 2:7, as in 2:24 and II John 5, 6, refers to the beginning of the Christian preaching, and thus to Jesus' own proclamation. However, in 3:11, where it also is said that "this is the message that you have heard from the beginning, that we must love each other," it is a different matter. Not only is reference made to Cain as a frightful example of hatred for one's brother and fratricide (3:12), but in addition, just before this, in 3:8, it is said that "the devil sins from the beginning." Thus it is an acceptable assumption that when he uses "from the beginning," the author is thinking not only of the beginning of the Christian preaching, but also of the beginning of all things.[19] It has to do with the "primal truth," the original, authentic, fundamental commandment. God has always intended and commanded that man should love his brother.

All his commandments come together in the commandment of love, and this commandment of love then branches out in a number of concrete directions. No one can regard himself as elevated above actual obedience to it. Love is not a matter of sentiments or of one all-dominating sentiment, very tenuous and spiritual, but of deeds—precisely as God's love for us was expressed in concrete deeds of Jesus (3:16; 4:10, 14). Hence love also can be commanded.[20]

In this connection it is important also to note how the author, who in 3:4-10 speaks emphatically of putting righteousness into practice and in verse 9 can say, "A child of God does not sin,

119

because the divine germ of life continues to be active in him; he cannot sin, because he is born of God,"[21] in verse 10 passes over directly from "doing righteousness" to "loving one's brother" and then comes out with the example of Cain. Therefore alongside 3:9 (cf. 2:29) can stand also 4:7b: "Everyone who loves is a child of God and knows God." Righteousness consists in the right relationship to God; righteous is the man who lets himself be guided and inspired by the way in which Jesus Christ is righteous (2:29; 3:7). Righteousness presupposes the keeping of the commandments and thus of the one great commandment of love. Precisely in his opposition to antinomianism the author guards himself against separating love and commandments.[22]

One Love with Many Aspects

In the foregoing, 2:5 has already been quoted: "But in a man who is obedient to God's word, his love actually reaches its perfection." What does the author mean by "his love"? The expression "the love of God" appears in I John several times and the meaning of "of God" is not always clear. The expression "the love of God" in 2:5 is parallel to "the truth" in 2:4. Is the author thus pointing to the love exhibited by God and inherent in God's being? Or does this refer to "the love toward God"? It is also possible to paraphrase it thus: "the love awakened by God," because love is of God ("comes from God") and everyone who loves is born of God ("is a child of God," 4:7), and one can also think of "the love that is willed by God," thus "love of divine quality."

Some texts speak plainly of God's love toward us, but then in what follows it always appears that the expression can signify still more. When after 4:9 all the emphasis is placed upon "loving one another," and it is said, "but if we love one another, God dwells in us and his love is made perfect in us" (4:12), then we must assume that the genitive here is not solely a subjective genitive. The same holds true when we read in 4:16: "Thus we have come to know the love which God has for us and to believe in it. God is love; anyone who abides in love abides in God and God abides in him" (see also what follows in 4:17, 18). Here love is a dynamic force which draws men along with it and enables them to love, in which man himself flourishes and bears fruit. One should also read 3:16, 17: "We have learned from Christ what love is: he has given his life for us. Thus we ought also to give our lives for our brothers. How then can the divine love abide in a man who has money enough and yet closes his heart against the need of his brother?" *God, who in Jesus Christ, saving and reconciling, has intervened in the world, is subject, source, and norm of all genuine love.* We are reminded of John 15, where love is spoken of in the context of the figure of the true vine.

God is also the object of love; I John twice speaks of loving God. Thus in the well-known text in I John 4:20-21: "If anyone says, 'I love God,' while he hates his brother, he is a liar. For if he does not love his brother whom he sees, he cannot love God whom he has never seen. This commandment then we have received from him: whoever loves God must love his brother also." Our loving God is so closely bound up with loving one's neighbor that the former is impossible without the latter, at least for Christians. In this connection it is worthy of note that in 4:11, "Friends, as God has so greatly loved us, we must also love each other," the link, "we must love him," is omitted from the argument. Of course this does not mean to say that for the author love for God and faith in God should be absorbed in or could be replaced by love for one's brother. It is true that over against the superspiritual and extremely religious people with whom he had to deal, the author found it necessary to underscore the actual character of love, directed toward the specific brother. But in his situation it was utterly inconceivable that he should be obliged or be able to speak atheistically (in our sense of the word) about Jesus and his disciples.

The exegesis of 5:1-3, where in connection with 4:20-21 the author speaks a second time of the relationship between loving God and loving one's neighbor, confronts us with some difficulties. Grossouw translates verse 2 as though it were giving a repetition of 4:21. "If we wish to love God and to keep his commandments, then we must also love God's children. This is our standard." However, another explanation of the Greek text[23] appears to me more acceptable. In this case the author is saying just the reverse: "We discern that we actually love the children of God by the fact that we love God and [thus] keep his commandments; for our love toward God consists in our keeping his commandments." It is true that against this interpretation it is argued that if this were the case, the author would be measuring a verifiable thing—brotherly love—with the help of a nonverifiable one—love for God. But this is not the way things are: the writer says twice, and thus emphasizes, that to love God presupposes the keeping of his commandments. One can no more genuinely love his brother without loving God than his love for God can be genuine without love for the brother.

The climax of the writer's exposition is formed by the declaration "God is love," which we find in 4:8 and 4:16. It is not that God *displays* a certain amount of love; he is not merely the source of all that may actually be called love: he *is* love. Here theology has reached the limits of its capacity of expression. After this utterance one would have to say a great deal or else keep silent. I confine myself to a few brief comments; the first two on this point I borrow from C. H. Dodd, who has found fitting formulations of them in his commentary on 4:8:

". . . If the characteristic divine activity is that of loving, then God must be personal, for we cannot be loved by an abstraction, or by anything less than a person. Thus even in using an abstract term the writer is not reducing God to an abstraction, since he is to be understood . . . as attributing to God an activity which is radically personal.''

With respect to the difference between the expressions ''God is love'' and ''God loves,'' Dodd remarks: ''The latter statement might stand alongside other statements, such as 'God creates,' 'God rules,' 'God judges'; that is to say, it means that love is *one* of His activities. But to say 'God is love' implies that *all* His activity is loving activity. If He creates, He creates in love; if he rules, He rules in love; if He judges, He judges in love. All that He does is the expression of His nature, which is—to love!'' To which Dodd then matter-of-factly adds: ''The theological consequences of this principle are far-reaching.'' [24]

Alongside ''God is love'' stand also ''God is light'' (I John 1:5) and ''God is spirit'' (John 4:24). Therefore, following the above reasoning, we must also say that God is wholly love, but his activity is not exhausted in loving. Thus we may never turn this expression around and declare that love is God.

This is forbidden also because in the expression ''God is love,'' not only God but also love is characterized. Apart from what the Christian community in faith has been able to see and to confess of God's activity in Jesus, it is simply impossible—according to the opinion of the author of I John—to say anything meaningful about love.

What Is Understood by "Brotherly Love"?

From the foregoing it has become evident that the author is writing as a Christian to people who to him are faithful Christians and in so doing sets himself against others who regard themselves as very good Christians but according to the author certainly are not. The expositions in I, II, and III John presuppose this situation and propose to answer the questions that arise herein and to unmask as false the answers given in this situation by the opposing party.

Does this imply that the author does not look any further than the community? The question becomes important especially if we wish to determine whom the author means by "the brother" and if in addition we explore how the word "world" functions with him.

For E. Stauffer the matter is perfectly clear: "Love between people is spoken of more often in the Johannine writings than in any other part of the New Testament. Here, however, the issue is not the love for one's neighbor, which Jesus preached, but love for one's Christian brother and comrade in the faith. The concept 'neighbor' does not appear at all in the writings of John, to say nothing of the commandment to love one's neighbor. Love has become an intra-churchly matter, and the church says: 'Love not the world' (I John 2:15)." [25] According to Stauffer this has more in common with the sectarianism of Qumran than with Jesus of Nazareth.

For Bultmann, however, the matter must be seen quite differently. In his recent commentary on the Epistles of John, he says on 2:9: " 'Brother' means, as in 3:15 and 4:20, not especially the Christian comrade in the faith, but one's fellowman, the 'neighbor.' " [26]

The truth appears to me to lie in between these two, though not precisely in the middle, as will become evident. It is clear that in 3:13 and III John 3, 5, 10, the word "brothers" has in mind members of the community. It is equally clear that the expression "to love the brother(s)" is used interchangeably with "to love each other" (see, for example, "brother(s)" in 3:10, 14, 15, 16, 17, in conjunction with "each other" in 3:11, 23). Similarly, in 4:7, 11, 12, "loving each other" is spoken of, but in 4:20, 21 it is "loving the brother." Thus in every case the brother is first of all the member of the community, the fellow child of God (5:1-2). In

124

view of the critical situation in which the author is writing, with the adversaries who look down on other Christians and have separated themselves from the community (2:19), it is not surprising that he hammers on just this one point.

Now is this, though, clearly a case where the saying "charity begins at home" applies, or is the author not looking further than the community, so that we must charge him with having a sectarian spirit?

Nowhere is brotherly love equated with what today is called human sympathy, or a feeling for other people. One can only presume that 4:21, with the close connection established there between loving God and loving one's brother, gives the Johannine version of the combination (reported in Mark 12:28-34 and parallels) of the two great commandments, and then remark, against Stauffer, that nothing here points to a restriction of the love of neighbor to the Christian community. And do not the example of hatred of one's brother chosen in 3:11-12, Cain's hatred for Abel, and the remark connected with it that the charge to love one another is a commandment which has been in effect from the beginning, make it impossible to think exclusively of relationships within the community?

But as some will say, is it not taught emphatically in 2:15-17 that one must not love the world? We do read in 2:15: "Do not lose your heart to the world or to the things of the world. If anyone loves the world, the love of the Father is not in him." And there are other texts also where "world" signifies the sphere of the anti-godly: 3:1, 13; 4:5; 5:4, 5, 19. Along with these we find texts in which the word "world" is used more or less neutrally, for example to indicate the stage upon which various events are enacted (3:17; 4:1, 3, 4; 4:17), but it is very evident that this neutral meaning can immediately turn into a negative one: thus, for example, in 4:1-6, where "in the world" is at once connected with "of the world," that is to say, "not of God."

125

There is, however, one text which clearly looks beyond the boundaries of the community to the world as the object of God's love. In 2:1b, 2, we hear: "But if anyone does commit sin, we have an advocate with the Father, Jesus Christ, who is entirely sinless, who makes expiation for all our sins, *and not only for ours but for those of the whole world*." The concluding phrase[27] reminds us at once of central affirmations from the Gospel of John, such as 1:29; 3:16; and 12:47; moreover, in I John 4:14, just as in John 4:42, Jesus is called the "savior of the world." Thus however much the author concentrates on the situation within the church, he does not lose sight of the fact that the whole world is the working area of God's love, and not only the small Christian community, where brotherly love must be put into practice. And thus he cannot have been of the opinion that brotherly love would not have to be continued in and expanded to love of neighbor. However, in his situation he found no occasion to speak of this.

Concluding Remarks

The concluding remarks need not be numerous. The exposition of love in I John is one-sided; various expressions in this epistle cannot be elevated to general truths and rules valid for all times and places—they are not intended as such. In this connection, however, I do not want to leave unmentioned a comment of K. Kohler about the detachment from the world which is commanded in the epistles: "If John in these critical days at the end of the first century had not reminded his people of the necessity of uniting for the purpose of mutual encouragement and for the strengthening of faith, perhaps we would not be here today to say, 'Let us love the men in the world.'"[28]

Furthermore, the seriousness of the situation prompted the author to think through the old truth anew and to translate it anew; he did not repeat the old, but allowed it to function anew. And it is given to him thus to penetrate to the heart of the matter. For him this heart lay in what was formulated in 1:1-4, the majestic prologue to the epistle; if he were able to speak among us today, he perhaps would utter again the words of verse 3 with which he began his epistle long ago: ''What we have seen and heard, we relate to you, so that together with us you may have a share in the fellowship which is given to us with God and with his Son Jesus Christ.''

IX

Jesus as Revolutionary

Introduction

The question about the man Jesus of Nazareth has in recent years become current in a new and unexpected fashion through the discussions about the so-called theology of revolution. What must be the attitude of the church in our time, which is marked by rapid changes in all areas of life? More specifically, what is the responsibility of Christians in situations in which revolutionary groups try to overthrow the established economic, social, and political order and in which violent revolutionary action appears to be the only possible way to bring an end to the injustice that is being practiced by those who have the power or that is inherent in the established social system? These questions are constantly being posed, and they are being posed urgently, because so many are being confronted with the necessity of making a concrete decision.[1]

In answering them of course an important role is played by the analysis of the biblical data which possibly could be relevant. Thus in the little booklet of the synod of the Dutch Reformed Church entitled *Revolutie en gerechtigheid* ("Revolution and righteousness"),[2] the concept of "righteousness" is given a central position. "Are there, in the revolutionary movements of our times, also certain tendencies coming to light which correspond to the righteousness which takes form in the coming of Jesus Christ from God?" Because Christians believe in the coming of the kingdom of God announced by Jesus and already dawned in him, in the victory of the righteousness that is both demanded and given by God, and in the realization of that righteousness on the whole earth, they cannot remain neutral, let alone react negatively, whenever in revolutionary action some aspect of that righteousness is striven for and realized. "Faith in Christ gives a vision of the time in which we work on new structures for our society. Hope signifies interpretation and rearranging of the facts. . . . The messianic thrust of the Old Testament and the gospel of Jesus Christ bring us anew to the discovery of the extremely revolutionary situation in which the world actually finds itself."

If one asks about what in the Bible can be normative for our theologizing and action as Christians in a revolutionary situation, then one naturally also asks about a possible revolutionary attitude of Jesus of Nazareth. May we call him a revolutionary? What was his relation to and his opinion of the revolutionaries of his time? The Jewish people, after all, lived under a Roman occupation, and in the Jewish literature of his day we hear repeatedly the cry for God's intervention and for the establishment of a world in which righteousness will actually reign.

Following what was written in the foregoing chapters, it is clear that in answering this question we must make a distinction between the pictures of Jesus as they are given in the Gospels and the rest of the writings of the New Testament, and what we can say on the basis of historical investigation about Jesus' attitude with respect to the revolutionary movements of his time. In the second place, we must not in bringing it up to date too easily adapt the insight gained through historical analysis to our own time. The question whether Jesus was a Che Guevara, a Camillo Torres, or a

Martin Luther King cannot be answered because it is mistakenly framed; it fails to recognize the great differences in the historical situation. In the third place, we must, naturally from the beginning of any investigation, clearly agree on what we mean by "revolution." With the above-named *Revolutie en gerechtigheid,* I choose the definition given by Arthur Rich:[3] "Under the term 'revolution' are understood all technical, social, and political changes which are brought about by people by design, in active involvement and in precipitous action, and which are marked by a new understanding of the whole of society." In answering the question as to Jesus' attitude, attention must be paid above all to the social and political aspects of revolution, the conscious striving for change in the institutions of society. At the same time it is necessary to devote special attention to the violent aspects, present not by definition (at least not according to the definition given above) but in fact, of a revolutionary struggle for social changes in the immediate future.[4]

It is remarkable that the question whether Jesus was a revolutionary is seldom posed in the ocean of publications about theology and revolution. When the New Testament scholars Martin Hengel and Oscar Cullmann in 1970 devoted publications to this question, under the titles *War Jesus Revolutionär.*[5] ("Was Jesus a revolutionist?") and *Jesus und die Revolutionären seiner Zeit*[6] ("Jesus and the revolutionaries of his time") respectively, they were able actually to mention only a little literature on the subject. From earlier times they cite publications of H. S. Reimarus, K. Kautsky, and R. Eisler,[7] and from recent times the journalistic book of 1965 by Joel Carmichael, *The Death of Jesus,* and the detailed book by S. G. F. Brandon, *Jesus and the Zealots,*[8] from 1967. Brandon's book is a sequel to his *The Fall of Jerusalem and the Christian Church* (1951),[9] in which he already defended the thesis that the Jerusalem Christians felt themselves closely allied with their countrymen in the fight for national independence; thus his investigation of the relationship of Jesus and the Zealots does not have to do directly with the recent discussion about theology and revolution, although his conclusions appear to be of great significance for this discussion.

In what now follows, the problem of whether Jesus of Nazareth was a revolutionary is approached in the first place by way of a critical review of Brandon's study of 1967. This is followed then, in order to illustrate the difficulties with which we are confronted, by the exposition of a biblical passage which is important in this connection, namely Mark 12:13-17 and parallels. Finally, I will attempt, primarily in connection with the observations of Hengel and Cullmann, to draw some lines from this historical investigation to the current problematic.

The Zealots

Brandon is of the opinion that Jesus' appearance in Galilee, in Judea, and in Jerusalem not only had unavoidable political consequences, but Jesus also deliberately aimed at an attack on the Jewish priestly aristocracy and thereby on the Roman overlords in Palestine. According to the inscription on the cross reported in all the Gospels, Jesus was put to death by the Roman authorities as "king of the Jews," and thus as a political figure—and from the Roman point of view there was reason for this: this man was dangerous; as in the case of so many of whom the Jewish historian Flavius Josephus tells, he was a troublesome rebel and a political revolutionary.

Brandon gives a detailed survey of the history of Israel in the years A.D. 6-73 and devotes a great deal of attention to the origin, the history, and the ideals of the movement of the Zealots.[10] Properly so, because possible political insights and activities of Jesus can be traced out and precisely evaluated only against the background of the concrete political situation of Palestine in the first century of the Christian era. We cannot treat the Jewish background in a separate section somewhere at the beginning and then for the rest speak only of Jesus' preaching and those separate stories about him in which one suspects a historical kernel, as is often done in the school of Bultmann; we shall have to answer the question of why Jesus was crucified by the Romans. Was this only a misunderstanding?[11] Every saying of Jesus and every story about him must be read against the concrete background of the (also sometimes politically) difficult situation of the Christian communities in the first and the beginning of the second century and against the background of the Jewish world of Jesus' day.

In this connection we must keep in mind the fact that any preaching about an intervention by God in earthly affairs in the future, even Jesus' proclamation of the kingdom of God, necessarily had a social and political character. The Jewish people's expectation of the future implied (and still implies) a total fulfillment of God's will, as laid down in his law, the Torah, upon earth. The Judaism of Jesus' day was anything but uniform; people thought differently about the way in which God's will had to be obeyed in the present and would prevail in the future. But the coming of God's kingdom always implies that God's will will be done, that the true believers will actually live righteously on a transformed earth under a righteous government, in genuine peace and prosperity. All injustice will be banished, and all resistance will be annihilated. There are varying ideas about the fate of those who do not believe; some see only the possibility of destruction or of utter subjection to the nation of the righteous that dwells around Mount Zion; others anticipate that those who do not know God will be drawn by his splendor and will come as pilgrims from all the ends of the earth to Jerusalem to join in worshiping him.

For Jesus, too, faith, ethics, and politics band together. But how? Brandon tries to show that on many points Jesus' ideas showed important aspects of agreement with those of the Zealots.

The most important source for our knowledge of the Zealots[12] is Josephus, and he was not favorably disposed toward them. Having gone over to the Roman camp in the Jewish War of A.D. 66-70, a protege of Vespasian and Titus, he attempts in his book on the Jewish War to explain how the revolt came about. Impressed by the Roman world power and even esteeming this in religious terms as a dominion willed by God (and there is no reason to accuse him of hypocrisy on this point), he wishes as much as possible to acquit the Romans of guilt. On the other hand he does not wish to place his own people in a bad light; hence his tendency to attribute all unrest in Palestine in the period from ca. 50 B.C. to ca. A.D. 66 to the activities of "bandits" and other radicals in the political and religious realm. His terminology varies, but is always derogatory. "Bandits" can be ordinary robbers, but the word used in the Greek *(leistai)* is also a kind of technical term for anyone who offers armed resistance to legal authority —depending on our perspective, we can label this latter category of people as guerrilla fighters, rebels, partisans, social radicals, or religious fanatics. There must undoubtedly have been chaff mixed with the grain; all sorts of motives must have played a part, but many were moved by *zeal for God's cause;* a zeal *(zelos)* to which they owe the name Zealots, a name which Josephus only uses for certain groups in A.D. 66-70 and then interprets in a negative way: "Thus [Zealots] they named themselves, as though they were pursuing noble aims and not the very worst of deeds and were not surpassing everyone else in such deeds."[13] The Latin term *sicarii,* "men who carry a dagger," assassins, was also used. Everything that was positive in the Zealots was brushed aside by Josephus: they are the evildoers; the Jewish people were peaceful (even though many were carried away in 66 partly because the last governors under Nero were utterly incompetent), and these peaceful folk can be regarded by the Romans as reliable. When the Jews, anywhere in the world, shall read Josephus' account of the

133

lost war, they will also dismiss from their minds any thought of coming to rebel again.[14]

It is not accidental that just after the Second World War more understanding arose for the positive side of the Zealots' striving. Historians are human, too! Brandon says (p. 24) that the English of the period 1850-1940 saw the Zealots with Josephus' eyes and regarded them as troublesome revolutionaries to be compared with the Irish, the Russians, or the Indians, but after 1939-1945 they knew what *Maquis* and partisans were!

Along with this we can also point to the important place which is held in the state of Israel as a symbol of national freedom by the last fortress captured by the Romans (in A.D. 73) from the Jewish radicals, Masada. The handsome photo book that the archaeologist and former general Yigael Yadin has published on the large-scale excavations of the settlement *(Masada, Herod's Fortress and the Zealots' Last Stand,* London, 1966) gives on page 202 a photograph of young Israeli military personnel who are taking the oath of allegiance up there on the plateau. The declaration "Masada shall never fall again!" appeared on special postage stamps and commemorative medals and was a battlecry in the June war of 1967.

We must see clearly that what we label with the modern words nationalism and patriotism was anchored for the Zealots in their interpretation of God's law. According to Josephus, Judas the Galilean, who in A.D. 6 called for a revolt when the Romans began to rule the territory of Herod's son Archelaus directly and for purposes of taxation organized a census, said: "God alone is our leader and Lord." Josephus, who summarily characterizes the stand and the behavior of this Judas as folly and draws the line directly to the Jewish War, underscores, however, the steadfastness and the readiness for martyrdom of Judas' followers who are willing to suffer anything so long as they do not have to call any man Lord. Therefore they resist the census, a sign of slavery, and call for resistance in the belief that God will help those who help themselves.[15] In other words, they wish themselves to realize with armed force the absolute lordship of God on earth, and they are ready to sacrifice themselves for the true theocracy.

Brandon portrays the Zealots with great sympathy and tries in a survey of the history of Israel from A.D. 6 to 73 to show how much the Zealots' ideals found response among the people. It has become a gripping story, which however cannot be acquitted of the charge of one-sidedness. In the first place we must not forget that not all *zelos* is zeal for God and his cause, "Zealot" *zelos*. I find the most appropriate example in the Assumption of Moses, a writing that dates from the beginning of the first century, which in the form of a prediction of the future by Moses gives an overview of the history of the Jewish people up to and including the sons of Herod and then passes over into genuine prediction. In the time of confusion and persecution just before the intervention of Michael, the angel sent by God, and of God himself, the mysterious figure of Taxo is brought on the scene, who says to his seven sons (after he has pointed to the disasters which have come upon the people and which are much worse than the disasters which have ever come upon godless people): "This is what we shall do: let us fast three days, and on the fourth day go into a cave which is in the field, and let us die rather than transgress the commandments of the Lord of lords, the God of our fathers. If we do this and die, then our blood shall be avenged before the face of the Lord" (Assumption of Moses 9.5-7). Here too is the typical zeal for the law of the Lord, not, however, coupled with guerrilla activity, but connected with fasting, prayer, stubborn defenseless resistance; if necessary, martyrdom, so that God, who determines that the measure is full, will intervene. I believe also that many of the prophets (branded by Josephus as charlatans and deceivers of the people) who led great numbers of the people into the desert were not trusting primarily in arms but in the miracles which God

135

would cause to happen there later, reminiscent of the days of Moses. Naturally the Romans suppressed these popular movements, and of course the people for whom Taxo was a symbol and an example, came to their end in a tragic fashion, but it is evident that in their zeal they had not chosen the side of the Zealots as did Judas the Galilean.

In the second place, it also is a major defect of Brandon's book that he nowhere goes into the political ideas of the Pharisees, who however were also zealous for a strict observance of the law and who in any case in the first half of the first century A.D. had a much greater influence among the people than did the Zealots. There were many ties between the Zealots and the Pharisees, and one can say that the former constituted the extremist left wing of the latter. Gedaliah Allon characterizes[16] the attitude of the Pharisees as follows: striving for political freedom, government by the people themselves; but realistically involved in the concrete possibilities of the moment; sometimes inclined toward cooperation with the Romans, for example where a Roman procurator—and relative internal autonomy—appeared preferable to a prince from the house of Herod; then again, as in 66, when the spark was put to the tinder, taking an active part with the radicals of the left; and finally, after the debacle, the diligent work of rebuilding under Jochanan ben Zakkai in Jamnia.

We need to consider all this when Brandon writes particularly about Jesus and the Zealots. Jesus could have been a stout Jew, standing for a radical interpretation of the law, a zealot in the true sense of the word—and yet no Zealot, not even when his preaching clearly had political consequences.

Jesus and the Zealots

Of course the accounts in the Gospels about Jesus himself are decisive, but these are in conflict among themselves. This discrepancy, says Brandon, is very simply to be explained: our earliest gospel, that of Mark, was written in Rome just after the triumphal entry of Titus in honor of his victory in the Jewish War. The Christians in Rome were obliged to give an explanation of the fact that their Lord was crucified as a rebel forty years earlier; Mark provides them with the arguments which they could adduce in their defense. Jesus was innocent; Pilate was convinced of this, but the Jewish leaders, especially the group around the high priest, pushed through the condemnation of Jesus.[17] The later evangelists, especially Matthew, go further along the way indicated by Mark. There we find the "pacifist Christ," for example in the beatitudes about the meek and the peacemakers (Matt. 5:5, 9), the words about hating and killing (5:21-23), the passage about revenge (5:38-41), or about loving one's enemy (5:43-48). We can also point to the story of the temptation in the wilderness (Matt. 4:1-11; par. in Luke 4:1-13, especially the temptation named by Matthew as the third) and to Jesus' word in Matthew 26:52 to the disciple who has cut off the ear of the high priest's servant: "Put up your sword, for all who take the sword shall perish by the sword." There is much more of the same tenor.[18]

It is fortunate, Brandon says, that Mark was not entirely consistent in his editing of the material which lay before him. He had before him a story that gives the view of the events held by the Jewish-Christian community in Jerusalem. This Jewish-Christian community was a para-Zealot organization; it believed in Jesus as a Jewish messiah and awaited his return. His martyrdom, through the conniving of the ruling high priestly party in Jerusalem —which later was also expelled by the "genuine" Zealots as soon as they got control of the temple in the days of the revolt—and at the order of the hated Romans, only accentuated the trustworthiness of his actions, his preaching, and his prediction of what should come. That the Messiah was put to death as a martyr was extraordinary, but after the experience of the resurrection people found proofs in the Scripture which rendered this death

137

acceptable.[19] Brandon tries thus to go behind the community theologies of the evangelists back to the earliest strata of tradition and by way of the oldest tradition—for him the presumed Jewish-Christian source—to trace Jesus' own intentions. Methodologically speaking, there is nothing against this (see chapter III), but there is the question whether Brandon's argument is consistent and whether his conclusions are probable. In the opening chapter of his little book Cullmann remarks that it is much too simple to distinguish two kinds of stories about and sayings of Jesus, namely those which more or less point in a Zealot direction and the positively anti-Zealot, and then to attribute one or another group of stories and sayings to early Christianity. He himself rightly defends the thesis that Jesus' attitude toward social institutions, the "establishment," without being intrinsically contradictory must necessarily have been complex, because his thinking was thoroughly marked by the anticipation of the imminent end of this age.[20]

Now if we inquire of Brandon's passages of proof for a Zealot attitude on Jesus' part, the most important ones appear to be the following:

1. Jesus had a Zealot among his disciples. Luke 6:15 and Acts 1:13 speak of Simon the Zealot, which Mark 3:18 and Matthew 10:4 conceal by calling Simon "the Cananean" (a grecizing of the Aramaic word). Does the surname indicate that he was a Zealot (and this in the sense of an adherent of the Zealot party?) or that he had been one? One should note that Matthew 10:3 also mentions Matthew the tax collector after it is earlier said of this disciple that he has abandoned his profession! Moreover, Jesus' association with the tax collectors and sinners, which then also was made an accusation against him,[21] was decidedly non-Zealot.

2. A very important point was the question of paying taxes to the Romans. We read about this in Mark 12:13-17 and parallels, a passage that comes up explicitly later on. It is good to see how

Brandon handles this story. Mark has used it to prove that Jesus conducted himself in a politically reliable way. But Jesus had meant his "give to Caesar what is Caesar's and to God what is God's" as any pious Jew had to mean it: the holy land and all that it produced belonged to God! Therewith Brandon makes Jesus out a Zealot. In Luke 23:3-5, then, the Jews say in their accusation before Pilate that Jesus is trying to lead the people not to pay taxes, inciting them to revolt, and calling himself Christ the king. Brandon cannot deny that with this account Luke intends to illustrate how the Jews deliberately place Jesus in a bad light, but yet he says that this account gives a very likely explanation. In so doing Brandon has made a circle, and he has found what he set out to find.[22]

3. The portrayal which the Gospels give of Jesus' behavior in Jerusalem provides various points of contact for Brandon's theory—at least this is the way he sees it.[23] He sees the entry into Jerusalem (Mark 11:1-10 and parallels) as a carefully planned messianic demonstration, a deliberate challenge to the Jewish and Roman authorities. The cleansing of the temple, which in the first three gospels follows the entry (Mark 11:15-19 and parallels), was an attack upon the temple aristocracy. Brandon rightly points out that the temple was not only a house of prayer, but also a bank and a business center and that the high priestly families and those connected with them represented a considerable economic force. It is likely that in this attack on the temple many more people were affected than the brief gospel narratives suggest, and the high priests and their like took this incident very seriously.

In any case, about the time that there was a disturbance about Jesus, there was a revolt in Jerusalem. In the story of Jesus' trial before Pilate there suddenly emerges the figure of Barabbas, the bandit *(leistes)*. Mark (15:7) says of him that he had been imprisoned with the rebels who had committed a murder during *the* insurrection (cf. Luke 23:19). Mark has nowhere earlier said that there had been an insurrection; thus he takes for granted that his readers know what is referred to, and/or he has faithfully taken over an earlier tradition in which familiarity with the insurrection was assumed. It cannot be proved, however, that Jesus was involved in this insurrection.

According to all the Gospels, at his arrest in Gethsemane (Mark 14:43-52) Jesus offered no resistance. But, says Brandon, Mark and the others do then tell that someone used a sword and cut off an ear! And in Luke 22:35-38 is preserved the curious story in which Jesus directs his disciples to sell all that they have in order to buy a sword and not to set out without a sword. When the disciples show him two swords, he says, "It is enough." Behind these scattered indications about the presence of weapons Brandon suspects more detailed stories about the use of weapons by Jesus' disciples. But we do not have these accounts, and in my opinion they are not to be found behind what is given in the Gospels. And if Jesus really had himself arrested, this represented a highly non-Zealot decision. His martyrdom is not that of many Zealots who fought to the death or, when taken prisoner after bitter fighting, let themselves be tortured to death; it resembles more that of Taxo in the Assumption of Moses.

4. Brandon dwells in detail on the accounts of the trial of Jesus before the Sanhedrin and before Pilate. These accounts are especially difficult to interpret because the distinctive view held by the evangelists of these events, so particularly central for the Christians in their discussion with the Jewish and non-Jewish non-Christians, placed a clear stamp upon the material which was taken over from earlier sources. Here for the sake of brevity I refer to H. van der Kwaak's recent study, *Het proces van Jezus* ("The trial of Jesus"),[24] which also devotes explicit attention to Brandon's views.

In any case, Jesus was crucified, and crucifixion was a Roman punishment, so the Roman governor must have played a part in the execution of Jesus. Jesus is crucified as a rebel. The inscription above the cross which identified him as "king of the Jews" is probably historical. Nowhere in the Gospels does the title "king of the Jews" play such a role as just in the accounts of the hearing before Pilate,[25] and it certainly was a title that was not very common in the early Christian community and one that was not without danger politically as well. The only evangelist who himself explicitly connects the title of king with Jesus and who seeks to explain the significance of this title is John, and he makes it entirely clear that Jesus had a kingship of a very special order. Jesus himself explains to Pilate what his kingship involves. His kingdom is not of this world; Jesus has come into the world in order, under a commission from God, to bear witness to the truth (John 18:33-38). Jesus is put to death on the grounds of a political accusation. Legitimately? One must at least reckon with the possibility of a misunderstanding, a mistaken comprehension of his actual intentions from the side of the priestly aristocracy in Jerusalem, from the side of the Pharisaic scribes, and from the side of the Roman authorities. The Gospels tell us that even Jesus' disciples understood his aims only poorly or not at all; must we then expect understanding on the part of outsiders? The situation was tense; there was no time for balanced thinking and extended investigation; action had to be taken. The Zealots will have viewed Jesus as someone who indeed spoke radically but did not act in a truly radical fashion. The leading group around the temple, precisely because they themselves were attacked by him, readily identified Jesus with the Zealot radicals. Many Pharisees were at odds with him on the point of his exposition of all sorts of prescriptions of the law, and they also were often more cautious, or in any case less radical, than Jesus in their expectations of the future. And we cannot expect of Pilate any understanding for any Jewish standpoint, especially when we consider the reports in Philo and Josephus of his conduct in Palestine.

Jesus' Eschatological Radicalism

Wherein now lies the uniqueness of Jesus' preaching? Cullmann rightly seeks this in the radicalism of his proclamation of God's kingdom. God's kingdom stands at the door, and it will speedily be fully actualized upon earth. From that perspective one must pronounce vigorous criticism on all striving for power among men—that of Herod Antipas, for example (Luke 13:32) and of the kings who have themselves called "benefactors" by their subjects (Luke 22:25). From thence comes the charge now to secure justice for all the oppressed and the outcasts of the earth and not to be attached to earthly possessions. From that perspective all religious tradition and all standard piety become in essence unimportant, and the possibility must be reckoned with that many will come from east and west to share in the kingdom with Abraham, Isaac, and Jacob (Matt. 8:11, par. Luke 7:9). A radical conversion is demanded of everyone who is serious about serving God (Mark 1:15).

As preacher of the imminent kingdom of God, Jesus has an attitude toward all that belongs to the "establishment" that is thoroughly critical. There is nothing established, nothing that stands firm for all times. Everything must change and will change, thanks to God's intervention. Man must order his life in accordance with this, and from it he must draw his own conclusions. But on the other hand the radical revolution which is imminent renders any conscious human striving for the reformation of the structures and institutions of society unnecessary and pointless. Who will busy himself for the overthrow of Roman power in Palestine if the days of that power are numbered? On the contrary, all the Zealots' striving is in fact an effort to lend a helping hand in a human manner, and as such is a temptation by the devil. "Seek first his kingdom and his righteousness and all this will be given to you as well" (Matt. 6:33). Nowhere then do we read either in the stories or between the lines that Jesus used violence or approved it. The cross is the radical no to all Zealotism.

Of course this sketch of Jesus' conduct must be amplified with an analysis of various central passages from the Gospels. There is no opportunity for such an analysis here. Something of that element, however, may be made clear on the basis of an exposition of Mark 12:13-17.

Give to Caesar What Is Caesar's and to God What Is God's

This brief story about the question of paying tribute to Caesar (Mark 12:13-17; Matt. 22:15-22; Luke 20:20-26) is a typical example of what Bultmann calls an apophthegm, a short story that finds its point in a saying of Jesus and therefore is handed on.[26] In Mark it is one of a series of disputes in Jerusalem which, along with the apocalyptic chapter 13, are placed between the story of the entry and the cleansing of the temple and the actual passion narrative. These facts are highly significant for the exposition of the story. In the first place, we must take into account the fact that we have to do here with a "typical story" shaped by the tradition, recording only that which is important as introduction to the saying of Jesus at the end. In the second place, we must also take into account the fact that the context in which this story now stands is constructed by Mark or by a source before Mark. We do not know at what moment in his career Jesus had this conversation; we do not even know with whom he had it. Mark (followed by Matthew) speaks of Pharisees and followers of Herod. He also names these together at the beginning of his gospel (3:6; cf. 8:15; *not* in Matthew) in an unholy alliance that had the aim of bringing about Jesus' death. This appears to be a peculiar touch of Mark.

By way of introduction Jesus' adversaries praise his truthfulness and his righteousness. He fears no one and he sees through people.[27] Then they pose the crucial question: Is it permissible to

143

pay tribute to Caesar or not? What is at issue is a direct tax (the Greek here uses the Latin word "census"), to be paid on the basis of a careful registration of people and property. Anyone who paid the tax acknowledged the right of the Roman emperor to levy taxes, and for the Jews of Jesus' time—one may recall what was said about the revolt under the leadership of Judas the Galilean —this was a much disputed matter. If Jesus issues a pronouncement about this, he puts himself under suspicion either with the radical group among the Jews or with the Romans. It appears that there is no other possibility.

However, Jesus does not let himself be caught; his answer becomes a question of conscience to his adversaries. First, so it is told, he has his opponents bring him a silver denarius. The denarii of the Emperor Tiberius bore the image of the emperor and the inscription: "Tiberius Caesar, august son of the divine Augustus." The adversaries have this coin in their hands when they say that Caesar's name and likeness stand on this coin—the questioners themselves have not in any case comported themselves as radicals.

Very well, then, says Jesus, give the emperor what is the emperor's, pay the tax which he demands in the coin which you now have in your hands, symbol of the political and economic order of the Roman Empire. And at the same time give God what belongs to God. Therewith the saying is taken out of its immediate context, and man is confronted with the fundamental question of what belongs to God and thus must be given to God. There are many explanations given of this saying: one could write a cultural history of Christianity on the basis of the various expositions of this text! Mark likely makes a connection between this story and one of the following conversations, that in 12:28-34 about the great commandment. When the scribe asserts that one should love God with all one's heart, mind, and strength, and one's neighbor as oneself, then Jesus says that he is "not far from the kingdom of God.'' In this fashion one ought to give God what belongs to God.

Now of course one may not infer Jesus' own intention in the saying from the context in which Mark places it. But much less may one establish, as Brandon has done, that of course Jesus shared the Zealots' viewpoint, that God is the only authority over the land and people of Israel, and that to pay taxes therefore is of the evil one. The Christians of the first generations, who found themselves constantly confronted by political decisions, did not themselves formulate this saying. Never and nowhere does it give a specific solution; it only penetrates to the fundamental question in every conceivable situation. Therefore an exposition which connects this saying with Jesus' words about the imminent coming of God's kingdom appears the most likely. God's kingship is confronted with the dominion of the emperor. There is no call for resistance to the emperor; he is destined to quit the field anyway!

Furthermore, there is no place provided for him alongside God; the ''and'' in Jesus' saying does not connect two commandments of equal weight. In the face of the intense expectation of God's kingdom and the firm confidence in God's conquering justice the emperor shrivels into an insignificant earthly lord. The real decision does not lie in the yes or no to the tax-collector, but in the yes or no to God, whose kingdom is coming.

Some Concluding Remarks

The question as to the Christians' attitude toward the revolutionary movements of this time cannot be answered exclusively by a reference to the attitude of Jesus of Nazareth as we think we are able to trace this out historically. There are other data in the Old and New Testaments and in any case a careful analysis of the manifold and confused situations in which revolutionary movements arise and operate is also necessary. Still the question can rightly be posed as to what the above historical sketch implies for those who in the present say yes to this Jesus of Nazareth and wish to follow him. Very cautiously and only as a partial response, I should want to answer that question as follows:

1. Christians ought to be agents of renewal by virtue of the vision given to them of the coming of the kingdom of God.

2. This kingdom includes a realization of God's justice and love, as these are preached by Jesus and are actualized already in him, on (a renewed) earth.

3. The expectation of the kingdom of God places men individually before the decision and calls them to a radical trust in God's possibilities.

4. It makes a person critical toward every human program of action that claims to bring fundamental renewal—even and precisely when these are identified as willed by God. With his "seek first God's kingdom and God's righteousness and all this will be given to you as well" (Matt. 6:33), Jesus is inspiring and disturbing presence at one and the same time.

5. Radical trust in the realization of God's justice by God himself led, in Jesus, to appeal, protest, prophetic action, and to the cross. And discipleship is to bear the cross. This means that for the Christian, violence, although perhaps sometimes unavoidable, is never defensible.

6. Cooperation with non-Christians in revolutionary actions and in other programs of renewal is possible only with a critical temper; but the Christians' criticism of others will always have to be combined with self-criticism.

7. In the *Ausblick* ("Prospect") at the end of his book, Cullmann points out that the fact that Jesus expected the revolution in a short time and we cannot simply follow him in this confronts us with a difficulty. We shall have to find a kind of alternation between the conversion of the individual (see 3 above) and changes in the structures (of which Jesus does not speak). But

precisely in this connection what was said in 4 and 5 remains valid.

8. In conclusion: the first Christians accepted the enigma of the cross and recognized the authority of Jesus' preaching and manner of life which led to this cross, on the grounds of the assurance that their Lord had conquered the forces of evil and of death. In this assurance they lived as a community, under commission from Jesus and trusting in the Spirit. In this assurance and trusting in the Spirit, people still, experimenting and correcting each other, may be confident that they will find the right words and may perform the right deeds, in an inspired obedience.

X

Who Are "We"?

Theologians and Tradition

"We have seen his glory"

John 1:14, "The Word became flesh and dwelt among us, and we have seen his glory, a glory as of the only-begotten of the Father, full of grace and truth," confronts us with many questions. Of all these questions posed by this important verse, I wish to treat only one: who are meant here by the word "we"?[1] This appears to be an incidental matter, but it is anything but that. An analysis of the use of the first person plural in this and some other sayings in the Gospel and the First Epistle of John sheds light on the Johannine view of the early Christian tradition. As is always the case with John, the exegesis compels us directly to consider one particular facet of Johannine theology. The study of this facet in turn compels us to study many other facets, and before we know it we are occupied from this perspective with the kernel of the Johannine utterance: the proclamation of Jesus as the Son who was sent by the Father and is uniquely related to the Father. In this way the discussion of the "we" in John can provide material for consideration of the question of who we ourselves are, we who ought to be concerned with what has been handed down to us and

148

who ought to be reflecting constantly on the question of whether and how this can be handed on by ourselves to people in our own times.

One thing is clear in John 1:14: the ones speaking here are believers who have been permitted and have been able to see the glory through the flesh. The Word was present in human form, but far from everyone perceived who was this Jesus of Nazareth who stood before them (cf. 1:12, 13). Not all seeing is believing seeing; that is to say, seeing that is inspired by faith and at the same time awakens this faith, strengthens it, and purifies it. Thus we read in John 6:14: "When the people saw the sign which he had done, they said, 'This is indeed the prophet who is to come into the world!' " Behind the miracles of the so-called multiplication of the loaves they detect a revelation. They come to a confession of faith, but still Jesus says to the same people when they come seeking him in Capernaum: "Truly, truly, I say to you, you seek me not because you have seen signs but because you have eaten the loaves and are satisfied" (6:26). A long discourse follows in which the deeper aim of Jesus' coming to the world, in his oneness with the Father, is proclaimed. The consequence is rejection, a crisis among bystanders and disciples. What there is to be seen remains concealed from many eyes; what is said is not understood. "Many of his disciples then heard this and said, 'This is a hard saying; who can hear it?' " (6:60). But in the end it is Peter who in the name of the twelve, on the basis of what they have seen and heard, confesses: "You have the words of eternal life; and we have believed and recognized that you are the Holy One of God" (John 6:69). Peter speaks of "we"; in view of the context, this word has primary reference to "the twelve." But is he not also a representative of the faith of the entire church?

With this question we are back again at John 1:14. Is it the eyewitnesses, those who had been present, who are speaking here, or is it the church? Or must we perhaps say: here eye witnesses are speaking in the name of themselves and of the church? To put it somewhat technically and theologically: have we to do here with a *pluralis apostolicus* (the "we" of the apostles) or with a *pluralis ecclesiasticus* (the "we" of the church)?

At this point it will be good to place alongside John 1:14 the introduction to the First Epistle of John. With an allusion to the prologue of the Gospel it is said there:

It existed from the beginning, we have heard it and have seen it with our own eyes; we have beheld it and our hands have handled it; about it we are speaking, of the word that is life.

For life has appeared, the eternal life that was with the Father has disclosed itself to us, we have seen it, we bear witness to it, we make it known to you. What we have seen and heard we communicate to you, so that together with us you may share in the fellowship with God and his Son Jesus Christ which is given to us. And we are writing to you in order to make our joy complete (I John 1:1-4).[2]

Of primary importance for our purpose is verse 3, where the "we" stands over against a "you." As is evident from the contents of the epistle, the you does not refer to outsiders, but to members of Christian communities whom the author wishes to admonish and to strengthen in their faith. Thus we cannot speak here of a *pluralis ecclesiasticus;* it is just as unlikely that we have to do here with a *pluralis majestatis,* because everywhere else in the epistle the author uses the first person singular. Must we then conclude that it is a *pluralis apostolicus?* (In this connection it ought of course to be pointed out that verse 3 does not prove that the author of I John was an eyewitness, in this case John the son of Zebedee, but it does show that the author[s] thought that he [they] might and must speak in the name of the group of eyewitnesses.)

The matter is not as simple as I John 1:1-4 seems to suggest. In

I John 4:14 we read: "And we have beheld and bear witness that the Father has sent the Son as Savior of the world." A clear parallel to I John 1:1-4, so it seems, but—in the context the "we" clearly means all believers. Just before this, for example, the sentence reads: "By this we recognize that we remain in him and he in us, that he has given us of his Spirit" (4:13). Now verse 14 begins with a quite emphatic "and we," and some have in fact assumed that by this word specific reference is made to a group of eyewitnesses. This exegesis appears to me less likely; but assuming that this were the correct meaning, then it is significant that the author uses the word "we" in one context in two different but obviously closely related senses. He could count himself as belonging to one group to which his readers do not belong, and when this idea emerges could address them as you. He can also refer to himself and this group together with his readers as we. We find the transition from the one to the other use of we in I John 1:5 and 6 where it first is stated: "And this is the proclamation which we have heard from him and proclaim to you: God is light and in him is no darkness at all," and immediately following this it is said: "If we say that we have fellowship with him and walk in the darkness, we lie and do not practice the truth."

The we's of verse 6 are clearly those addressed plus the author; indeed we need to draw the circle even somewhat more widely; when those addressed say something of this sort, they say this together with the false preachers against whose influence this epistle is warning (see also 1:8, 10; 2:4, 6, 9). If "we" say this, says the author, then our life is a lie. It can be remarked that this is only a tactical use of the plural: unnumbered preachers through the centuries must have said we when they meant you, because people more easily accept something from someone who places himself in a line with them than from someone who sets himself opposite them or above them. But at least this use of the plural is not prompted solely by tactical considerations, but also by feelings of solidarity, of belonging together. And in I John still more is involved.

I come back once more to I John 1:3. The translation by Professor Grossouw is more flowing and more modern than that of the Dutch Bible Society, but it fails to bring out clearly one point which does come out well in the Bible Society's translation: "That which we have seen and heard we proclaim to you, that you also might have fellowship with us. And our fellowship is with the Father and with his Son Jesus Christ." We must note the order, which is essential for our purpose: so that *you* might have fellowship *with us;* and *our fellowship is with the Father and with his Son Jesus Christ.* To put it in modern jargon: the vertical relationship comes into being via the horizontal. Not only is the horizontal relationship of brotherly love essential,[3] but also, and even in a very special sense, the horizontal relationship of the connection with the past generations and with the eyewitnesses at the beginning of the chain of tradition. The emphatic reference of the author of I John to the fellowship with the eyewitnesses as an indispensable link in the fellowship with the Father and the Son issues from the polemical situation in which he is operating. This is portrayed in detail in chapter 8. John is dealing with adversaries who place great emphasis upon their own spiritual existence and on their exalted fellowship with God. Over against these people there is need to hold fast to the "fleshliness" of Jesus Christ (cf. John 1:14) and to the impossibility of coming to know God in any other way than through him. Anyone who wishes to know him is referred to the testimony of those who have seen and heard him; more precisely said, those who have been permitted to see in him "the eternal life that was with the Father" (vs. 2).

Thus the eyewitnesses belong organically to the fellowship of the church; thus the church is organically connected with the eyewitnesses and through them with Jesus and with God. What is involved here is not only solidarity, an experience which allows

152

later generations as it were to share belatedly in what happened earlier. What is essential is the trustworthy tradition from generation to generation in which the eyewitnesses from the past have a fundamentally different function from that of the believers in the present, and in which the believers in the present are referred, for their relation to God, to their relation to the eyewitnesses.

Now that we have arrived at this point, it will be good to return once more to the Gospel of John. At the end of chapter 21, which ought to be regarded as an appendix to the gospel, we meet a group who express it as their conviction that the testimony of the disciple whom Jesus loved is true; referring to the content of the entire gospel (not merely of chapter 21; cf. the "of these things" in 21:24 with "these [things]" in 20:31) it is said: "This is the disciple who testifies of these things and who has described them, and we know that his testimony is true" (21:24). Those who are speaking here obviously form a second link in the tradition process; when they recognize the trustworthiness of their spokesman as witness, they recognize at the same time their dependence upon this testimony (cf. also 19:35, which probably belongs to the same phase in the editing of the Gospel: "And this one has seen and has borne witness to it, and his testimony is true and he knows that he speaks the truth, so that you also may believe").

The so-called first ending of the Gospel of John underscores what we have just found. In John 20:30-31 there is mention of the many other signs which Jesus had done "before the eyes of his disciples" and which are not described in this book; and of all that is written the reason is given: "that you may believe that Jesus Christ is the Son of God and that believing you may have life in his name." What was done was seen, accepted in faith, and testified to. This testimony was handed on and even written down, with the aim of awakening and strengthening faith.

In this connection it is necessary to devote a few words to the story of Jesus' appearance to his disciples and especially to Thomas in 20:24-29 which concludes with Thomas' confession of faith, "My Lord and my God!" and with the word of the risen Lord to Thomas: "Blessed are those who have not seen and yet believe." This utterance immediately precedes the just-discussed first ending of the gospel. For this reason alone it is unlikely that here a believing that is not based on seeing is to be more highly regarded than a believing that is based on seeing. Instead, this rather is spoken over Thomas' head to those who, unlike him, will not be able to refer back to their own experience. According to the conception of the Fourth Gospel, Thomas' fellow disciples have earlier been allowed to see what now is shown to Thomas (20:19-29), and even of the beloved disciple it is said, even with a certain emphasis, "he saw and believed" (20:8). The Christians who are not among the eyewitnesses, however, are referred to the word of the eyewitnesses. Thus we read in the so-called high priestly prayer: "And I pray not only for these *but also for those who believe in me through their word,* that they all may be one, as thou, Father, art in me and I in thee, that they also may be in us" (John 17:20).

On the basis of what has just been said, we must affirm that the "we have beheld his glory" in John 1:14 in any case is grounded in the seeing by the eyewitnesses. However, 1:16 proves that this utterance need not be limited to the eyewitnesses' seeing; there it says, "Out of his fullness we all have received even grace upon grace." "We all" are obviously all believers, not only the people of the first generation; but it is made clear by the form of the Greek verb that is used that it has to do with an event in the past which is not repeated at every moment. The "seeing" of the eyewitnesses is the basis of their bearing witness and of all the church's speaking. The *pluralis apostolicus* passes over into the *pluralis ecclesiasticus,* and the *pluralis ecclesiasticus* is inconceivable without the *pluralis apostolicus.* With all the distinction there remains in John's view an organic connection. And that connection can best be identified with the word "tradition," tradition understood in the sense of a living process of handing-on.

In this connection attention needs to be fixed for a moment on the central role which the Gospel of John assigns to the Holy Spirit in the period after Jesus' departure. One should read the farewell discourses in John 14-17, and in particular the passages that appear there about the "Paraclete," "the Holy Spirit, whom the Father will send in my name," of whom it is said: "This one will teach you all things and will bring to your remembrance all that I have said to you" (John 14:25, 26; cf. 14:15-18; 15:26-27 and 16:7-14). In order for the eyewitnesses to learn to recognize what is essential in what they have heard and seen, they need the guidance of the Spirit. The Spirit bears the tradition; he reveals nothing new, but causes that which is seen and heard to be perceived as God intends it, even in totally new situations. Thus for example in 12:16, with reference to the entry into Jerusalem, where the evangelist refers to Zechariah 9:9, it can be said: "At first the disciples did not understand this, but when Jesus was glorified, then they remembered that this was written about him and that this had been done to him" (cf. 2:22 and 20:9). Thus the entire Gospel is a large-scale attempt to translate under the guidance by the Spirit that which is handed down in the tradition for a new situation. Thus the epistles intend to combat certain views which can be seen as misapprehensions, not by clinging to the old formulations, but by a rethinking of the old in response to the problems posed by the adversaries. In the Johannine circle it was known that what is traditional is reliably and responsibly handed on, not by repetition, but by constant reinterpretation and reformulation.

It is evident that still much more could and must be said about this. I limit myself to one last comment. Just as the first person plural can be connected with various groups, the word "you" in the farewell discourses also denotes the disciples to whom Jesus is addressing himself directly, as well as all believers who in the time after his departure will live in union with him. In John 14:25 it refers to the disciples who are present: "These things I have spoken to you while still remaining with you." In verse 26, which speaks of the Holy Spirit, the disciples are incorporated into the larger circle of the church: "He will teach you and bring to your remembrance all that I have said to you." The disciples play a unique role, but they play it within the larger whole as members of the great fellowship of believers.

Who Are We Ourselves?

It is time now to pass from exposition to application. I address myself in particular to the situation in which theologians now find themselves, but hope that nontheologians will read on through this and will discover that theologians too are only ordinary people. Whenever they wish to be Christians, they are, by virtue of their specialty, confronted with all the difficult questions with which believers in this present time must come to terms.

Who are we ourselves? Often we are somewhat split personalities. On the one hand we stand within the tradition process, and will—most of us—call ourselves believers and stand ready for the personal engagement that is called for by texts such as John 20:31. On the other hand, our commission to be practicing theologians in a scholarly way brings with it the obligation to regard the traditional with a critical eye, from a certain distance, and likewise to take a critical stance with reference to the manner in which the traditional is being handed on and actualized, in the churches and without, by groups and by individuals. This brings with it an inner tension with which we must learn to live, however difficult this can be for some at certain moments. This tension is healthy, both for our faith and for our scholarly work.

156

Those who regard the linguistic and historical approach to the past as a disfiguring of the sacred tradition, especially of that part of the tradition which is clothed with authority as Holy Scripture, need to consider that in any process of tradition there lurks the danger of hardening and narrowing, and that living out of the tradition often leads to our finding ourselves in the tradition without our actually having listened to the past. Precisely through the application of modern, strictly historical methods can what was said in the past be understood as the expression of living faith; and what is situated in this fashion in an earlier context can sometimes open up unsuspected vistas in the present. Among the driving forces in the renewal movement, which in the Roman Catholic Church in our day is leading to such radical changes, is the scientific study of the Bible according to the generally accepted methods and a new engagement with the church fathers. A critical approach to the traditional can be serviceable to the process of tradition in surprising fashion, so long as limits are not set for this approach in advance by the church's authority, by the consensus that prevails in a certain circle and the social pressure that is coupled with it, or by one's own pious mind.

No Disinterested Theology

At the same time it is clear that theology cannot limit itself to linguistic and historical investigation. The very object of this investigation compels us to study the tradition in later stages and to reflect on the question of a responsible interpretation in the present. The theologian who specializes in the area of the historical critical investigation of a particular part of the tradition needs to be aware of the larger whole within which his work is performed, of the responsibility which he bears within that whole, and of the decisions with which he himself as a man is confronted. To study theology in detachment is impossible. The *pluralis apostolicus* passes over into the *pluralis ecclesiasticus,* and the

157

investigator cannot avoid answering the question of whether, and if so, in what way, he makes this latter ''we'' his own. And if, in spite of and with his critical objections, he says ''we,'' this signifies that he knows himself to be incorporated into a great, immense, highly mixed, and sometimes not very attractive group of people over the whole world who also say ''we.'' Perhaps he feels like someone playing on the left wing, but he is still a member of the team, and for the playing of the game he is committed to cooperation with his teammates. The author of the First Epistle of John makes the charge against his superspiritual opponents that they have separated themselves from the church(es) and over against the spiritual ''we'' are setting the ''they'' (perhaps we could better say, the ''you'') of the ordinary church people. This is why in his plea for love he hammers on the theme of brotherly love. This plea warns theologians against the constant temptation to regard themselves as better than the church folk, along with bishops, local church councils, and synods.

A following remark is connected with the statement that for John tradition involves reinterpretation and reformulation. Here I should like to give a long quotation from an article, ''Theologie en cybernetica'' (''Theology and Cybernetics''), by Dr. J. M. de Jong.[4] In that article he writes:

Would it not be better to abandon the tiresome schema of an *eternal content* or truth and a regrettably *timebound form,* in order to arrive at the insight that God has coded his unique information in a form which is not so much ''timebound'' as ''time-oriented,'' a coded document, the Bible, that may and must be decoded ever anew? And this indeed because in the meantime, while through ''feedback'' information is admitted from the changing outside world and from the course of the centuries, the coded ''output'' also changes? This change then is no relativizing of the original account, but the very thing that guarantees its constancy in changing times. For to say the same thing in changing times and circumstances, one needs to say it differently. Is that not the activity of the Spirit, that is to say, of God himself, who makes himself contemporary with the present? Time will have to teach us to what extent the elements which are added to our language by cybernetics . . . have or do not have any meaning for the forming of theological concepts. I suspect that this will be the case, because of the mobility and exactness of these elements of language in which the factors *time* and *interaction* are incorporated,—something that cannot be said of all forming of theological concepts.

Theologians will have to have a thorough knowledge of the times in which they live and will even have to share intensely in these times for themselves. In the program of study a large place will have to be made for orientation to our own time, precisely so that the process of tradition can find continuation in responsible fashion. It remains essential, however, that the same theologians learn to evaluate the earlier formulations of "God's unique information" in their proper function and significance.

This raises the question of how we shall be able properly to assimilate all this. One can take too much hay on his pitchfork or be choked with a superficial knowledge of many things and thereby neither arrive at an actual encounter with the present nor come to a genuine study of the past. Of course specialization is necessary, but it makes sense only when one engages in it on a broad foundation.

Teamwork

Here one can and must insert the word "teamwork." Teamwork of teachers, especially between those of the specialties oriented to the past and to the present, and interdisciplinary cooperation is also necessary. Teamwork of students, who must be trained also to work together in church and society in groups with differently oriented theologians and with people from other disciplines. Teamwork of teachers and students: this implies an arrangement of theological studies different from the one that is

159

common at present, and a diligent search for this new model is going on everywhere. It will be difficult to arrive at a new design, not only because of the diversity of views, but also and especially because of the difficulties inherent in the material itself. Some want a new pattern of education alongside or replacing the existing one, in which subjects such as dogmatics, ethics, philosophy of religion, and anthropology would have to be the central subjects, and special care would have to be devoted to the study of sociology and psychology as well as to practical training. Church history and the history of religions would get relatively little attention and the biblical subjects could be studied without an acquaintance with the original languages. Various things are suggested in order that theology in the twentieth century can be an "answering theology" and so that the theologian, in an education that bears a dialogical character, can learn how the tradition in which he stands can function in the world of today. The problem is properly stated; the discussion of the practical solutions will be lengthy precisely because no one wants a more intense confrontation with the present to be gained at the expense of an actual immersion in the past; what do we have in a highly modern functioning of the *pluralis ecclesiasticus* if the essential bond with the *pluralis apostolicus* is lost?

I break off here; it would take us beyond the limits set for this volume to deal further with the problem of theological study in the university. Besides, John's "we of the church" has in mind not only, and not even in the first place, the theologians. Therefore we now consider some comments on the task of the so-called laity and the collaboration between theologians and non-theologians.

Some Notes on the So-Called Layman

It Refers to All Believers and the Entire World

We cannot say, I believe, that the current interest in the place of the layman in the church issues directly out of a new discovery of the central place of the ordinary member of the community in the New Testament view of the church. Various factors will have played a role here: the world appeared to have changed, the necessity of renewal of the church's life and change in the church's method of work and organization was evident—and then people discovered that in the Bible all sorts of ideas were to be found, indeed were even very central, ideas which people previously had not taken very seriously. As is so often the case, there has been an interaction between the reflection on change in the culture and the study of the Bible.

What then have we discovered anew in the Bible? We cannot think of giving here a complete summary of relevant biblical motifs, but a few main lines can be drawn.

1. The church is the people of God, a fellowship called, set apart by God, to serve him and to be an instrument for his work in the world. It is not a matter of favored individuals, but a fellowship that is constituted and governed by God's voice. God forms an agreement (covenant) with the people of Israel. They must serve and worship God, must be different from other peoples, so that it can become evident to everyone that God the Lord is different, that he rules the whole world, and that he demands of everyone on earth a particular obedience.

2. The obedience to the Lord ought to be manifested in the entire life of the fellowship that is called by him. No separation may be made between especially sacred areas of life and society and a number of profane, secular sectors. One need only read the ten commandments to realize that trust in the Lord who delivered the people out of Egypt is determinative for the whole life of both fellowship and individual. It was not for nothing that Israel also gave form to its distinctiveness by obedience to the Sabbath commandment and by observance of the dietary laws. The New Testament offers different emphases, but in essence nothing is altered: "You are the salt of the earth" (Matt. 5:13); "You are the

161

light of the world'' (Matt. 5:14); ''Let this mind be in you which was also in Christ Jesus'' (Phil. 2:5). Passages like the Sermon on the Mount and the hortatory chapters of Paul's epistles make it clear that God's Love in Christ intends to renew the whole man and leaves no facet of human society out of consideration.

3. It is self-evident that in this view of service to God every believer, as a member of the fellowship, has a task. It is the ordinary members of the congregation who form the church, not only at the time when they come together to pray, to sing, to speak, and to eat (the Supper was originally also an ordinary meal), but also whenever anyone is at work in his place in the world. In the world, but not of the world; not of the world, but in the midst of the world; strangers, but not alien to the world.

In this connection, in the Bible the believer is first of all seen not as an individual, but as a member of the community. It is not up to Mr. A-all-by-himself to try to be a genuine Christian in the particular situation in which he functions daily, but the community, believing in the Holy Spirit, will have to see his service and his witness as part of the common service and the common witness. It will have to draw from this the conclusion that it, the community, as a whole is also responsible for what the man does there—that it must help him, think through his problems with him, share his joys, and possibly determine with him that this profession or occupation is not reconcilable with a Christian life (and then set about to find another job for and with Mr. A). The admonitions in the New Testament always presuppose a fellowship which takes them to heart, and the promises also are realized within the community. Of course there is the personal appeal, the summons to personal choice, but when Paul is converted, there is a community in Damascus that receives him; we can imagine what the words of Ananias to Paul (Acts 9, especially verse 17) meant: ''Saul, brother, the Lord has sent me''! Whenever we presently expect much of the layman, who stands in the breakers, on the dividing line between church and world, and place high demands upon him, we must be sure to see that this assumes a renewal of the concrete life of fellowship in the churches. Only out of a living fellowship which can be seen, felt, and experienced, with mutual services rendered in a spiritual and a material regard, can the individual believer actually serve, as a stranger who is not alien to the world, with God's help in God's cause.

4. In the association between God and people in the Old Testament various people play a mediating role. Moses, the great mediator between God and people, according to Old Testament and later Jewish views occupied a unique position: "I speak with him mouth to mouth, plainly and not in obscure speech, and he beholds the form of the Lord" (Num. 12:8). After him there are the prophets and the priests, the judges and the kings, the teachers of wisdom and the scribes, sometimes holding an office on the basis of their belonging to a certain tribe (the priests from Levi) or family (the kings from the house of David), sometimes unexpectedly called for a particular task (the judges, many of the prophets). The office and the commission always apply to the people, the community, in order that God's plan for this people, this community, can be realized.

In the New Testament, again, the case is not essentially different from that in the Old Testament. (In view of the churches' discussions of office and church order, we might feel obliged here to provide a full demonstration of the unique position of the twelve apostles and of the unique phenomenon, that the New Testament has no knowledge of priests as functionaries within the community; but I shall leave this aside for now.) Ephesians 4 speaks a plain language here: Paul addresses the entire community on the fact that they are called to a very particular manner of life, in love and unity. Within the one body, governed by the one Spirit, the individual gifts are given "to equip the saints for the work of ministry, for building up the body of Christ" (4:12).

163

Thus the whole community will be able to grow in love and power, so that the truth can be preached and lived; lived in and before the world which is the ultimate object of God's concern.

Theologians and Nontheologians

The discussion of the task of the layman in the church has many sides. Here I limit myself to the question as to the function of the theologian in the religious fellowship and (connected with this) that of the theological schooling of the ordinary church member. A few remarks on these questions:

1. The second great commandment demands of us, among other things, that we serve God with all our mind. I know that the Greek word used here denotes a broader field of spiritual activity than the intellectual alone; and it is very clear that obedience to God must make us very critical of our own wisdom. But throughout the Old and New Testaments it is said that service to God calls for the commitment of the whole mind. Our thinking is not disengaged, but is directed by and toward God.

2. To serve God with the mind is the task of every believer. This thinking is not addressed solely to religious problems: in principle it covers all areas of life because, as was said earlier, the Bible knows no separation between the secular and the religious in a human life. Of course it will not be allowed to stop at thinking; individual and corporate deeds must follow.

3. This Christian thinking and acting assumes a clear insight into the problems with which people are confronted (thus objective information) and great love, nourished by trust in God, coupled with clear insight into what God has thus far revealed to men concerning his intentions for man and world. It is the modest but, in the larger whole, indispensable task of theology to reflect upon God's intention for man and world. This demands a certain specialized knowledge, for example of the history of religions, of the content and backgrounds of the Bible, of trends of thought and

life experiments in church and world during the past nineteen centuries of Christendom, and so forth. Addressed to a very special object, theology also makes use of a particular specialized language. This is self-explanatory: in any specialty people make use of a specialist's language because certain things can be said only in a certain unique way.

4. In theology much attention is devoted to the past. Understandably so; we stand in the present, but in the tradition of centuries. God's concern with people has not begun just today, and we shall have to study again and again just the crucial moments of this concern of which the Old and New Testaments tell us. But theology becomes a genuinely living, current activity only when we venture to draw the line to the present and the future.

And this is not a task for theologians alone. They can contribute building stones. They can say "this is how it was" or "this is the way this or that must be understood"; or "Careful! At such-and-such a time people also tried that, and later it appeared that they had taken a wrong road." The theologians may and must impart to the ordinary church members the most essential things from the Bible and church history and so forth. The layman must not be satisfied with broad but superficial talk about religious matters. The layman will have to perceive that certain typically biblical words and theological terms are actually irreplaceable. Of course we shall have to translate them ever anew, and shall have to take care that they continue to be living words and not linguistic fossils, but as we do this, we shall remain concentrated always on the essential content of these words and concepts. The theologian, however, remains suspended above the world and fails to make contact with the present if he does not strive, in collaboration with the nontheologian and in continuing conversation also with non-Christians, to speak in contemporary terms and to find guidelines for contemporary Christian action. Theology in isola-

165

tion is no theology at all; only in a persistent and patient thinking together and talking together of theologians and ordinary church members will the church as a whole be able to come in our world to the point where it speaks responsibly and acts surprisingly. By means of Jesus, the inspiring and disturbing presence, God calls us all, theologians and laymen, to make a contribution, to the benefit of both the church and the world, to an authentic contemporary theology and to experiments in Christian action which are joined to that theology.

Notes

Chapter I

1. See Paul Rodenko's selection of Gerrit Achterberg's poems, *Voorbij de laatste stad,* Den Haag/Antwerp, 1955, p. 122.

2. See R. L. K. Fokkema, "De varianten van Vergeetboek," in the issue of *Maatstaf* (Vol. 11, No. 10/11, Jan./Feb., 1964) dedicated to the memory of Gerrit Achterberg, pp. 771-86; see also "Voorbeelden van varianten," pp. 787-94.

3. Following *Voorbij de laatste stad,* Den Haag, 4th ed., 1965, p. 175, and Gerrit Achterberg, *Verzamelde gedichten,* Amsterdam, 1963, p. 922.

4. Nederlands Bijbelgenootschap, Amsterdam, 1st ed., 1964, 4th ed., 1967.

5. See F. Visser, "Catechiseren met de foto's uit *Licht,"* and M. de Jonge, "Catechiseren met het evangelie van Johannes," in *Theologie en Praktijk,* XXIV, 1964, pp. 180-85 and 166-79 respectively.

6. See *Licht* again at this passage.

7. J. A. T. Robinson, *Honest to God* (Philadelphia: Westminster Press, 1963).

8. A. N. Wilder, *Early Christian Rhetoric* (New York: Harper & Row, 1964).

Chapter II

1. The original version of this chapter appeared as an article under the title, "Het kerkelijk gesprek en het gesprek tussen kerk en wereld," in *Theologie en Praktijk,* XXIII, 1963, pp. 76-92.

2. See "Stellingen bij het richtingsvraagstuk," published in *Kerk en Wereld,* March 13, 1959, p. 2.

3. Nijkerk, 1957 [Communication of the Christian Faith] (Philadelphia: Westminster Press, 1956).

4. *Nederlands Theologisch Tijdschrift,* XIII, Feb. 1959, pp. 206-15.

5. Eugene Nida, *Message and Mission* (New York: Harper and Brothers, 1960).

6. *Ibid.,* p. 221.

7. *Ibid.,* p. 222.

8. *Ibid.,* p. 226.

9. *Ibid.,* p. 228.

10. *New Testament Studies,* VIII, 1961-1962, pp. 101-16. The passage quoted is on p. 106.

11. Paul Minear, *Images of the Church in the New Testament* (Philadelphia: Westminster Press, 1960). This book is a contribution to the discussion in the Theological Commission on Christ and the Church instituted by the department of Faith and Order of the World Council of Churches.

12. *Ibid.,* p. 252.

13. *Ibid.,* p. 251.

14. "Verdrongen of bedwongen verlegenheid," *Wending,* XVII, pp. 576-85.

Chapter III

1. The original version of this chapter appeared as an article in *Wending,* XIX, 1964-1965, pp. 718-32.

2. Albert Schweitzer, *The Quest of the Historical Jesus* (New York: Macmillan, 1906), p. 5.

3. *Ibid.,* p. 399, 400.

4. *Geschichte der Leben-Jesu-Forschung,* p. 640.

5. Rudolf Bultmann, *Jesus and the Word* (Naperville, Ill.: Allenson, 1959), p. 8.

6. London: SCM Press, 1972, pp. 541-68 (this book is a written version of lectures given in 1932-1933).

7. K. Barth, *Protestant Theology in the Nineteenth Century* (Philadelphia: Judson Press, 1973), pp. 565-66.

8. Rudolf Bultmann, "The Primitive Christian Kerygma and the Historical Jesus," in *The Historical Jesus and the Kerygmatic Christ,* tr. and ed. Carl E. Braaten and Roy A. Harrisville (Nashville: Abingdon Press, 1964), pp. 24-25.

9. See M. de Jonge, "Enige recente studies over het leven van Jezus," *Theologie en Praktijk,* XV, 1955, pp. 97-111, which discusses five English "Lives of Jesus" from the period 1950-1955.

10. Robinson, *A New Quest of the Historical Jesus,* pp. 9-10.

11. (s-Gravenhage, 1962.)

12. As most important I mention Ernst Käsemann, Günther Bornkamm, Ernst Fuchs, and Gerhard Ebeling. For more detailed information see the book (difficult for nonspecialists) by James M. Robinson, cited in note 10, above.

13. Gerhard Ebeling, *Theology and Proclamation: A Discussion with Rudolf Bultmann,* trans. by John Riches (London: Collins, 1966), p. 71.

14. See Ebeling, *Theology and Proclamation,* pp. 65 and 49-54.

15. Ernst Käsemann, *New Testament Questions of Today,* transl. by W. J. Montague (Philadelphia: Fortress Press, 1969), "The Beginnings of Christian Theology," pp. 82-107; "Blind Alleys in the 'Jesus of History' Controversy," pp. 23-65. He also gave new inspiration to the pursuit of the quest of the historical Jesus by his article, "The Problem of the Historical Jesus," in *Essays on New Testament Themes,* transl. by W. J. Montague (London: SCM Press, 1964), pp. 15-47. This article appeared first in *Zeitschrift für Theologie und Kirche,* 51, 1954, pp. 125-53.

16. Cf. I John 4:1-3.

17. E. Käseman, *New Testament Questions of Today,* p. 50. Käsemann concludes: "The measure of faith, then, was not ill-chosen. It has always been binding within Christendom and I think it must always be so in the future."

18. Cf. Paul van Buren, *The Secular Meaning of the Gospel* (New York: Macmillan, 1963), pp. 117-26. Among other things, he states: "The believer was called to test his understanding of, and his response to, every concrete situation in life, by reflecting on the history of Jesus" (p. 125).

Chapter IV

1. *Wending,* XVIII, 1963-1964, pp. 758-70.

2. And one should read in addition the illuminating exposition by Oscar Cullmann in his *The Christology of the New Testament,* transl. by Shirley C. Guthrie and A. M. Hall (Philadelphia: Westminster Press, 1963), pp. 247-48.

3. Robinson, *Honest to God,* p. 74.

4. Dietrich Bonhoeffer, *Letters and Papers from Prison* (New York: Macmillan, 1971), pp. 381-82.

5. Bonhoeffer's thoughts in *Letters and Papers from Prison* are, in the nature of the case, fragmentary and his terminology is provisional; one does not find a completed system here.

6. It is quite significant that in the discussion in the Bultmannian school the accent has shifted from the negative demythologizing to the positive existential interpretation.

7. Robinson, *Honest to God,* p. 49.

8. The discussion with Robinson on this point will unavoidably develop into an intensive discussion with Tillich; see, for example, his *Systematic Theology,* Vol. II, pp. 5-18.

9. For a more detailed treatment of this, see chapter 2.

10. See the variant reading in Matt. 19:17.

11. See also Robinson, *Jesus and His Coming* (London: SCM Press, 1957).

Chapter V

1. Albert Camus, *The Fall,* transl. by Justin O'Brien (New York: Alfred A. Knopf, 1957), pp. 114, 112, and 113.

2. The original version of this chapter appeared as an article in *Theologie en Praktijk,* XXV, 1965, pp. 198-212.

3. See also Chapter 4, the section headed "Robinson's Valid Points."

4. Wilder, *The Language of the Gospel: Early Christian Rhetoric* (New York: Harper & Row, 1964), p. 65.

5. Oscar Cullmann, *Salvation in History* (New York: Harper & Row, 1967), p. 143.

6. Wilder, *The Language of the Gospel,* pp. 20-25.

169

7. *Ibid.,* pp. 17-18. Fuchs' term may be translated as "language-event." Its full meaning becomes comprehensible, as do those used by Wilder, only in the context of the broader exposition of their thought by these writers. On this point, at least with respect to Wilder, see especially chapter 6.

8. *Ibid.,* p. 37.

9. *Ibid.* This is treated in more detail in chapters 3 and 6.

10. *Ibid.,* p. 90.

11. Van Buren, *The Secular Meaning of the Gospel* (New York: Macmillan, 1963), p. 156.

12. *Ibid.,* p. 147.

13. *Ibid.,* p. 199.

Chapter VI

1. The following is a revision of an article, "De traditie en Jezus," which appeared in *Theologie en Praktijk,* XXVII, 1967, pp. 1-18. Much of what has been treated in the preceding chapter has been omitted here.

2. One should also read by Wilder: "Eschatological Imagery and Earthly Circumstance," *New Testament Studies,* V, 1958-59 (New York: Cambridge University Press), pp. 229-45; "Form-history and the Oldest Tradition," in *Neotestamentica,* ed. by W. C. van Unnik and B. Reicke (Leiden, 1962), pp. 1-13; and "The Word as Address and the Word as Meaning," in *The New Hermeneutic,* Vol. II of *New Frontiers in Theology,* ed. by James M. Robinson and John B. Cobb, Jr. (New York, Evanston, and London: Harper & Row, 1964), pp. 198-218.

3. The basic meaning of koinònia is sharing in something, "partnership"; see J. Y. Campbell, "Koinonia and its Cognates in the New Testament," in *Three New Testament Studies* (Leiden, 1965), pp. 1-28.

4. This is the main issue in the discussions between Jesus and the Jews in chapters 5 through 10.

5. R. Schnackenburg, *The Gospel According to John,* Volume I, Introduction and Commentary on Chapters 1-4, transl. by Kevin Smyth (London: Burns and Oates; New York: Herder and Herder, 1968), p. 511.

6. The form-critical approach has already been discussed in chapter 3. In redaction criticism an attempt is made through comparison of the Gospels to arrive at an indication of what is theologically distinctive about each of the Synoptics. W. Marxsen, in his *Introduction to the New Testament,* transl. by G. Buswell, (Philadelphia: Fortress Press, 1968), pays a great deal of attention to redaction criticism. Other important books include: H. Conzelmann, *The Theology of St. Luke,* transl. by G. Buswell (New York: Harper and Brothers, 1960); W. Marxsen, *Mark the Evangelist: Studies on the Redaction History of the Gospel,* transl. by James Boyce, et al. (Nashville: Abingdon Press, 1969); G. Bornkamm, G. Barth, and H. J. Held, *Tradition and Interpretation in Matthew,* transl. by Percy Scott

170

(London: SCM Press, 1963); and W. Trilling, *Das wahre Israel: Studien zur Theologie des Matthäus-Evangeliums* (München, 3rd ed., 1964).

7. Thus, for example, Martin Dibelius, *From Tradition to Gospel,* transl. by Bertram Lee Woolf (Greenwood, S. C.: The Attic Press, 1971), p. 184: "That here God's will had been done, all who knew the Risen Lord guessed and, indeed, knew. It was proved for them by the Old Testament." In this sense see also R. Bultmann, *The History of the Synoptic Tradition,* pp. 283-84, where he speaks of dogmatic motives which have affected the passion narrative.

8. Wilder, *The Language of the Gospel,* pp. 37-38.

9. On p. 21, Wilder says: "Jesus was a voice not a penman, a herald not a scribe."

10. Wilder, *The Language of the Gospel,* p. 48. Wilder here is opposing the views of H. Riesenfeld (in "The Gospel Tradition and Its Beginnings," *Studia Evangelica,* TU 73, Berlin, 1959, pp. 43-65) and B. Gerhardsson (in *Memory and Manuscript,* Lund/Copenhagen, 2nd edn., 1964), according to whom Jesus' teaching exhibited many formal points of agreement with that of the scribes. This view fails to do justice, he says, to "the eschatological outlook of Jesus who was not schooling his followers in a learned mode for new generations to come, and the intense urging with which he spoke to the immediate crisis and the face-to-face hearer." (*The Language of the Gospel,* p. 23; cf. pp. 23-25; 49-51; 63-64). This point appears to me to call for closer examination.

11. Wilder, *The Language of the Gospel,* p. 24. Wilder concludes from this: "Here is one of the touchstones not only of Christian literature but of the Christian arts generally." It may be noted here in passing that Wilder, although of course he, like many others, tries to get back to the earliest stages of the tradition and to the words spoken by Jesus himself, relativizes the question of historicity. With reference to the parables, in which people have thought that to a great extent they could get back to Jesus' own words, he says (p. 90): "We have a natural desire to identify precisely his authentic words, the *ipsissima verba.* The importance of this should not be overestimated. We can know Jesus historically through the eyes and through the hearts of his immediate followers even if they do not remember his words exactly and even when they quite understandably adapt, supplement and generalize them, not to speak of those which they forget or pass over. Even when they put words in his mouth these, too, may convey to us the reality of the founder in what is most essential. Jesus' creative speech was so fresh and significant that it could, as it were, breed speech true to itself. We have an analogy of this phenomenon when we say that certain stories about Abraham Lincoln may not be authentic, but they are true to Lincoln."

12. Wilder, *The Language of the Gospel,* p. 56: "What makes such stories and such dialogue so formidable is that in each one God, as it were, forces us to give him a face-to-face answer, or to look him in the eye."

13. Wilder, *The Language of the Gospel,* p. 67.

14. "The historical Jesus comes into better focus if we see him as using two media to proclaim the kingdom—in addition to his action, of course. On the one

171

hand he used eschatological imagery and categories. 'The kingdom of God is at hand.' He spoke of judgment, the Messianic banquet, the life of the age to come, perhaps of the Heavenly Son of Man coming with the clouds of heaven. All this was available theological symbol of his time and place. But he said the same things in what we call layman's language in his parables of the Kingdom, parables of judgment, etc. What does this mean except that he brought theology down into daily life and into the immediate everyday situation? Here is a clue for the modern preacher, indeed for the Christian whatever his form of witness." Wilder, *The Language of the Gospel*, p. 94.

15. *Ibid.*, p. 124.

16. *Ibid.*, chapter 7, entitled "Image, Symbol, Myth" (pp. 126-36).

17. *Ibid.*, p. 131.

18. *Ibid.*, pp. 133-34, 135.

19. If we may at least assume that Jesus spoke this story in some form. On this, see, for example, J. Jeremias, *Die Gleichnisse Jesu* (Göttingen, 7th ed., 1965), pp. 67-75; and B. M. F. van Iersel, *"Der Sohn" in den synoptischen Jesusworten* (Leiden, 1961), pp. 124-45.

20. See H. J. Held, in "Matthew as Interpreter of the Miracle Stories," in *Tradition and Interpretation in Matthew,* by G. Bornkamm, G. Barth, and H. J. Held, transl. by Percy Scott (London: SCM Press, 1963), pp. 219-20, 253-59.

21. Matthew has this story also (15:32-39), but Luke has incorporated into his gospel only the feeding of the five thousand (9:10-17).

22. Thus, among others, James M. Robinson, *The Problem of History in Mark* (Naperville, Ill.: Allenson, 1957), pp. 84-85.

23. Thus, among others, E. Best, *The Temptation and the Passion: The Markan Soteriology* (Cambridge, 1965), pp. 179-80, and M. Karnetzki, "Die galiläische Redaktion im Markus-evangelium," (ZNW, 52, 1961), pp. 238-72, especially p. 245.

24. In 7:27 Jesus says, "Let the children be satisfied first." In both of the stories of feeding the throngs it speaks of "satisfying" (6:42 and 8:8).

25. See chapter 4, pp. 64-65; cf. also chapter 2, pp. 26-27.

26. Cf. J. M. de Jong, *Kerygma* (Assen. 1958), especially 151-63.

27. In R. Bultmann, *Jesus Christ and Mythology* (New York: Charles Scribner's Sons, 1958), p. 69, he says: "First, only such statements about God are legitimate as express the existential relation between God and man. Statements which speak of God's actions as cosmic events are illegitimate."

28. Van Buren, *The Secular Meaning of the Gospel*, p. 141. This new perspective is bestowed at Easter. "When Easter is the centre of the picture, however, we can then say that the meaning of the Gospel is to be found in the areas of the historical and the ethical, not in the metaphysical and the religious" (p. 197).

29. One more quotation from A. N. Wilder's *The Language of the Gospel:* "The word of God found its appropriate vehicles both in the sense of images and forms. Within limits one can say that to this very day and always Christianity will most characteristically communicate itself at least in these three modes: the drama, the narrative, the poem—just as it will always be bound in some degree to its primordial symbols, no matter how much the world may change" (p. 51).

Chapter VII

1. This chapter is a revision of an article which first appeared as "Communication in Words and Silence," in *The Friends' Quarterly*, XV, 1965-66, pp. 268-76.

2. Heinrich Böll, *Eighteen Stories*, transl. by Leila Vennewitz (New York: McGraw-Hill, 1971), pp. 118-49.

3. I found this quotation (dated in 1937) in *Christian Faith and Practice in the Experience of the Society of Friends*, 244 (1961).

Chapter VIII

1. This chapter is a revision of a lecture given at Leiden on February 10, 1968, in the context of the observance of the anniversary of the founding of the University of Leiden. It appeared earlier as an article under the title, "Geliefden, laten wij elkander liefhebben, want de liefde is uit God (I Joh. 4:7)," in the *Nederlands Theologisch Tijdschrift*, XXII, 1967-1968, pp. 352-67. It is included in the present volume because it shows how in I John speaking about God and speaking about Jesus are directly related and how confession is directly connected with a life in and from love.

2. Eltheto-brochure, *Geloven met je handen*, Zeist, November 1967; the passage quoted is found on pp. 15-16.

3. See G. Th. Rothuizen, "Enige kritische beschouwingen over de Nieuwe Moraal, in het bijzonder met het oog op John A. T. Robinson," *Vox Theologica*, XXXVII, 1967, pp. 238-51, especially pp. 243 ff. The other contributions in this issue of *Vox Theologica* are also worthwhile.

4. This example is borrowed from J. Fletcher, *Situation Ethics* (Philadelphia: Westminster Press, 1966), p. 116.

5. Robinson, *Honest to God*, p. 116. On this book, see further chapter 4, above.

6. Robinson, *Christian Morals Today* (Philadelphia: Westminster Press, 1964).

7. Fletcher, *Situation Ethics*, p. 70.

8. See Fletcher's first chapter. Antinomianism is a life-perspective which refuses to be subjected to laws or fixed rules; legalism is a life-perspective which gives first priority to a strict obedience to laws and fixed rules.

9. Fletcher, *Situation Ethics*, p. 158.

10. These facts are taken from R. Morgenthaler, *Statistik des neutestamentlichen Wortschatzes* (Zürich-Frankfort a.M., 1958).

11. *Agape* appears 7 times in the Gospel of John (67 pages), 75 times in Paul (157 pages), and 21 times in the Epistles of John (12 pages). The verb *agapan* appears 36 times in the Gospel of John, 33 times in Paul, and 31 times in the

Epistles of John. If one divides the number of occurrences by the number of pages, one gets the following percentages: *Agape:* the entire New Testament, 17 percent; the Gospel of John, 15 percent; Paul, 48 percent; the Epistles of John, 175 percent. *Agapan:* the entire New Testament, 21 percent; the Gospel of John, 54 percent; Paul, 21 percent; the Epistles of John, 251 percent. For other writings the proportional figures are still less favorable than for those cited.

12. "L'aspect moral de la théologie johannique a été très peu étudié" ("The moral aspect of Johannine theology has been given very little attention"), thus the beginning of the "Introduction" of N. Lazure's *Les valeurs morales de la théologie Johannique* (Paris, 1965, 387 pp.).

13. Dodd, *The Johannine Epistles,* London, 1946, pp. XXI-XXII.

14. For many exegetical details and for the reconstruction given here of the position of the Christians which the author is opposing, reference may be made here to M. de Jonge, *De brieven van Johannes* (Nijkerk, 1968).

15. One should note the many instances in this epistle where the indicative and the imperative appear side by side.

16. It nowhere appears that the opponents are thought to have abandoned themselves to dissipation and to have led a dissolute life; the only specific sin with which they are charged is that of lovelessness toward their brethren.

17. In the translation by W. K. Groussouw *(De eerste brief van Johannes, Nieuwe vertaling met korte uitleg,* Boxtel: K. B. S., 1963), the phrase "from the beginning," which in the Greek belongs with the "have had," is added to "the word which you have heard"—evidently for stylistic reasons.

18. Cf. also II John 4-6. Verse 4 speaks of walking *in the truth,* just as we have received a commandment from the Father; verse 5 speaks of the *commandment* which we have had from the beginning, namely the commandment to love one another; verse 6 then speaks again of walking according to God's *commandments,* immediately followed by a reference to *the* commandment. In John 14:21, 23, 24, Jesus speaks in succession of "my commandments," "my word," "my words," and "the word which you have heard," which is not actually "my word," but the word "of the Father who has sent me."

19. Cf. also II John 1:1 and 2:13, 14.

20. In his *Gospel and Law* (Cambridge, 1951), C. H. Dodd says of the Christian *agape:* "It is not primarily an emotion or an affection; it is primarily an active determination of the will. That is why it can be commanded, as feelings can not" (p. 42).

21. A very difficult verse, in which the author goes to the extreme of what he can say on the basis of the "now, already."

22. N. Lazure (pp. 226-29) makes an illuminating comparison between the Johannine literature and Deuteronomy. In both sources one can speak of the "amour-alliance," because there is in both a close connection between loving and keeping the commandments—one should read, for example, Deut. 30.

23. One should let the *en toutoi* point forward and connect it with the following *hotan.*

24. Dodd, *The Johannine Epistles,* pp. 109-10.

25. *Die Botschaft Jesu damals und heute* (Bern, 1959), p. 47.

26. Bultmann, *The Johannine Epistles,* transl. by R. Philip O'Hara with Lane C. McGaughy and Robert W. Funk (Philadelphia: Fortress Press, 1973), p. 28.

27. The words in italics are lacking in the parallel text 4:10.

28. *Le Coeur et les Mains* (Neuchatel, 1962), p. 77.

Chapter IX

1. For a good balanced analysis of the problem see *Revolutie en gerechtigheid,* a "Nota" of the Raad voor de Zaken van Overheid en Samenleving (i.e., "council for matters of government and society"), issued by the synodal board of the Nederlandse Hervormde Kerk (the Dutch Reformed Church; s'Gravenhage, 1969). For a bibliography, see this Nota, pp. 77-78, and R. Hensen, "Informatie terzake van een theologie der revolutie," *Theologie en Praktijk,* XXIX, 1969, pp. 19-29.

2. See note 1. The following quotations are to be found on pp. 15, 47-48.

3. See Arthur Rich, "Theologie en revolutie," *Wending,* XXIII, 1968-69, pp. 245-63; definition on p. 247.

4. On this see especially *Revolutie en gerechtigheid,* pp. 18-23.

5. Martin Hengel, *Was Jesus a Revolutionist?* transl. by William Klassen (Philadelphia: Fortress Press, 1971); Hengel's inaugural address at Erlangen, supplied with many and detailed notes.

6. Cullmann, *Jesus and the Revolutionaries,* transl. by Gareth Putnam (New York: Harper & Row, 1970); a revision of a lecture delivered on November 4, 1969, at the Faculté Libre de Théologie Protestante in Paris, at the opening of the academic year.

7. For Reimarus (1778), see Schweitzer, *The Quest of the Historical Jesus,* chapter II; and for Kautsky (1908), see the German edition of 1926, *Geschichte der Leben-Jesu-Forschung,* pp. 576-77. R. Eisler created a great stir with his *Iesous basileus ou basileusas,* I and II, Heidelberg, 1929-30. Brandon made critical use of it, and it was followed in a popularizing way by Joel Carmichael. On Eisler see also H. van der Loos, *Jezus Messias-Koning,* Assen, 1942.

8. S. G. F. Brandon, *Jesus and the Zealots* (Manchester, 1967). The same author's *The Trial of Jesus of Nazareth* (London, 1968) presents the same portrayal of Jesus' conduct as does the book cited in the text.

9. Brandon, *The Fall of Jerusalem and the Christian Church* (London, 1951).

10. *Ibid.,* chapters 2 and 3.

11. "This death can scarcely be understood as an inherent and necessary consequence of his activity; rather it took place because his activity was misconstrued as a political activity"—thus Bultmann in "The Primitive Christian Kerygma," p. 24.

12. Along with Brandon's book, one should read the solid work by Martin

Hengel, *Die Zeloten* (Leiden-Köln, 1961), and W. R. Farmer's suggestive *Maccabees, Zealots and Josephus* (New York, 1956).

13. Josephus, *The Jewish War*, IV, 160-61.

14. See, for example, M. Hengel, *Die Zeloten*, pp. 6-18.

15. See *The Antiquities of the Jews*, XVIII, 1-10, 23-25.

16. In "The Attitude of the Pharisees to the Roman Government and the House of Herod," *Scripta Hierosolymitana*, VIII, 1961, pp. 53-78.

17. See Brandon, *Jesus and the Zealots*, chapter 5.

18. *Ibid*. See chapter 6.

19. *Ibid*. See chapter 4.

20. *Jesus and the Revolutionaries*, p. 12.

21. See the saying, probably an ancient one, in Mark 2:16.

22. See Brandon, *Jesus and the Zealots*, pp. 270-71, 345-49.

23. *Ibid*. See chapter 7.

24. H. van der Kwaak, *Het proces van Jesus* (Assen, 1969). Van der Kwaak discusses Brandon's theories on pp. 87-96.

25. We also encounter the title of "king" in the account of the entry into Jerusalem (though not in Mark). One should also consult here the book by O. Betz, *Was wissen wir von Jesus?* (Stuttgart-Berlin, 1967), especially pp. 56-63.

26. See also chapter 6, in the section headed "How did people speak of Jesus?" Vincent Taylor prefers to use the category of "Pronouncement-story."

27. The common translation, "You do not pay attention to the position of men," seems to me not to be correct for Mark and Matthew (though it is for the different expression in Luke). The Greek expression used corresponds to that in the Greek translation of I Sam. 16:7: "Man looks at what is before his eyes, but the Lord looks at the heart." The adversaries were correct, Mark suggests; Jesus unmasked their hypocrisy, indeed, and saw through them just as God sees through men.

Chapter X

1. The first part of this chapter, "Theologians and Tradition," presents a revision of the text of the opening lecture which was given on September 18, 1968, before the theological faculty at Leiden. It appeared earlier under the title, "Wie zijn 'wij'? Enige beschouwingen over het gebruik van de eerste persoon meervoud in het evangelie en de eerste brief van Johannes," in *Theologie en Praktijk*, XXVIII, 1968, pp. 169-80. The second part, "Some Notes on the So-Called Layman," was taken from the brief essay, "Enige bijbelse notities," in an issue devoted to "the so-called layman" of the *Mededelingen der Barchembeweging* (XXXVIII, 1964, pp. 1-6).

2. This follows the translation of Grossouw; see chapter 8, note 17.

3. See chapter 8.

4. This is now in the volume (issued posthumously) *Voorrang aan de Toekomst* (Nijkerk, 1969), pp. 149-68; the quotation appears on p. 166.